LA BELLE

MEMOIRS OF COURT AND SOCIETY
IN THE TIMES OF
FRANCES TERESA STUART
DUCHESS OF RICHMOND AND LENNOX

BY
CYRIL HUGHES HARTMANN
M.A., B.Litt

LONDON
GEORGE ROUTLEDGE & SONS, LTD.
NEW YORK: E. P. DUTTON & CO.
1924

Printed in Great Britain by
F. Robinson & Co, at the Library Press. Lowestoft

LA BELLE STUART
Sir Peter Lely. Hampton Court Palace

[*Front.*

TO CYNTHIA

PREFACE

Despite the prominence in her own time of Frances Teresa Stuart,* Duchess of Richmond and Lennox, no attempt to write a full-length biography of her seems hitherto to have been made. It is true that the more important incidents in her career have frequently been described in works on the Restoration period, and short accounts of her have appeared in books dealing with the Court of Charles II; but no writer has as yet ventured to go beneath the surface and analyse her character in any detail. The omission is undoubtedly due to the fact that posterity has been content to accept the contemptuous opinion of her expressed by the author of the Gramont memoirs, and has consequently decided that it would be waste of time to make anything in the nature of a psychological study of her.

It is because, rightly or wrongly, I disagree with the generally-accepted opinion of La Belle Stuart that I have decided to write this monograph. It has been one of my chief aims to confine my narrative as closely as possible to the Duchess and her affairs, and to avoid digressing to such an extent that my heroine would

* In my own allusions to Frances Stuart I have followed the mode of spelling the name invariably used by the Blantyre Stuarts and by the Duchess herself (cf. pages 230 and 235). The original spelling in contemporary references has, however, been left unchanged.

appear as but one of many flies caught in a web of Stuart history. I have endeavoured to restrict allusions to contemporary affairs, both social and political, to such as helped to form an appropriate background to my central figure.

The book has been compiled mainly from contemporary sources, both printed and manuscript, and I have depended as little as possible on later writers. At the same time I have to confess that many laborious hours of research have been saved for me by writers who have gone over the same ground, and I feel that I should acknowledge my debt to such works as Baillon's 'Henriette-Anne d'Angleterre,' Forneron's 'Louise de Keroualle,' and Miss Davidson's 'Catherine of Bragança.' But as a general rule I have gone back to the original authorities, which I found chiefly in the British Museum (Add MSS., Egerton MSS. and Stowe MSS.), the Record Office (Calendars of State Papers—Domestic and Foreign, and Treasury Books, etc.), and the Archives of the French Foreign Office, where I studied the volume containing Charles II's letters to his sister, and many volumes of despatches from the French ambassadors in England. These are referred to in the text under the heading of C.A. (Correspondance Angleterre). The remainder of the sources from which I drew information are indicated in the foot-notes.

In addition to these more or less easily accessible authorities there was a certain amount of material in private hands, and here I had to rely entirely on the kindness and courtesy of those in whose power it was to give me help and information. In this respect I have been most fortunate, having experienced the most generous consideration, from all whose help I sought. It would be impossible, indeed, to thank individually all who have helped me, especially as some of my greatest obligations were incurred when I was investigating possibilities which yielded no results. In a book of this kind I considered it unnecessary to exhibit the bare bones of fruitless research, so that no record appears of unsuccessful investigations.

One of the most formidable tasks was the writing of the brief appendix on the portraits of the Duchess. Even now I do not pretend to be in the least satisfied with it; it can at best be regarded as a hook baited to attract further information. I had gracious permission to view the Huysman portrait in the private apartments at Buckingham Palace, and other owners offered me like facilities, of which I availed myself whenever possible. When that was impracticable I was given full descriptions of the pictures and their history, so far as it was known. I also had invaluable advice in determining their authenticity from Mr J. D. Milner, Director of the National Portrait Gallery, Mr Ernest Law, C.B., Mr Long, of the South Kensington Museum, Mr C. H. Collins Baker of the National Gallery, and my uncles, Mr Talbot Hughes and Sir Herbert Hughes-Stanton, R.A. But it should be clearly understood that, except when otherwise stated, I accept full responsibility for all opinions expressed.

In regard to MSS. in private hands; my thanks are due to Sir Harry Verney, Bart., who kindly allowed me to make a search among the Verney Papers at Claydon House, and to the Marquess of Bath, K.G., who provided me with two important letters hitherto unpublished. The Lennoxlove Papers afford almost the only available details about the latter part of the Duchess's life. Major W. A. Baird, who inherited the estate from his grandfather, the last Lord Blantyre, placed these documents at my disposal and was throughout most untiring in his assistance. The Lennoxlove portraits of the Duke and Duchess of Richmond are reproduced by his permission, and the Gascar portrait of the Duchess by permission of the Duke of Richmond and Gordon K.G., at whose hands I experienced great courtesy.

I cannot adequately express what I owe to the inestimable advice and thoughtful criticism of Lady Helena Carnegie, whose knowledge and understanding of the past are an inspiration to others as well as to herself, and whose vivid sympathy and unfailing encouragement have intensified for me the great pleasure of writing this book.

CONTENTS

Page

CHAPTER I

Restoration of Charles II.—Return of the exiled Royalists—Frances Stuart's birth and parentage—Her upbringing at the Queen-Mother's Court—Princess Henrietta married to the Duke of Orleans—Projects for the marriage of Charles II—The Infanta of Portugal chosen—Frances appointed a Maid of Honour—Madame's letter introducing her to Charles II—Arrival of Catherine of Bragança—Marriage of the King—The honeymoon at Hampton Court—The Queen's household—Charles appoints Lady Castlemaine a Lady of the Bed-chamber—His quarrel with the Queen—Clarendon's intervention—Catherine's reconciliation with Lady Castlemaine—Peace at Court 1

CHAPTER II

Royal entry into London—Frances Stuart's friendship with Lady Castlemaine—The King falls in love with her—Gramont's opinion of Frances—Her beauty—The story of the green stockings—Arrival of Cominges—His contempt for the English Court—Charles II. and Frances—Report of a mock-marriage—The Duke of Monmouth's wedding—The Court Ball—The Marquis de Ruvigny—Lady Castlemaine's quarrel with Frances and its settlement—The Queen and her ladies riding in the Park 24

CHAPTER III

The Court at Tunbridge—Frances in the ascendant—Her many admirers—Buckingham—His character and career—His attempt to govern the King through Frances—Mary, Duchess of Richmond—The Butterfly story—Buckingham's party for the King—Sir Henry Bennet—George Hamilton—He ingratiates himself with Frances—Interference of Gramont—The Court at Oxford—Lady Castlemaine's illness—The Court returns to London—Frances Stuart's virtue—Schemes to procure her for the King—She is advised by her mother and Henrietta Maria—The Queen's illness—Her hallucinations—Charles continues to make love to Frances—Talk of his marrying her in the event of the Queen's death—Lady Castlemaine's conversion—Charles II's reply to her indignant relations—Recovery of the Queen—Charles still determined to make Frances his mistress 42

xi

CHAPTER IV

Charles dons a black wig and resumes his pursuit of Frances—His offers to her rejected—His divided love—Lady Castlemaine's effrontery—Rumours collected by Pepys—Anglican sermons—Frances resists the King—Miss Jennings—The story of the calash—Portraits of Frances—The Comet of 1664—Predictions of the astrologers—War with the Dutch—The célèbre ambassade extraordinaire—Courtin turns his attention to Frances—The Great Plague—The Court retires to Hampton Court—Lady Castlemaine departs to Richmond—Lely's 'Beauties'—The King and Queen at Salisbury—Frances Stuart's dream—Charles II in Dorset—Parliament meets at Oxford—The breach with France—Strained relations between the King and his brother—Intrigues against Clarendon—The Court returns to London—General belief that Frances is the King's mistress—Clarendon's opinion—The Court in mourning—Tunbridge again—The Great Fire of London—The Persian mode introduced—Ball at Whitehall . . . 67

CHAPTER V

The King's persistence—Frances contemplates marriage—The Duke of Richmond—His character—He proposes to marry Frances—Lady Castlemaine betrays them to the King—Frances appeals to the Queen—Charles affects to countenance the match—The elopement—The King's anger—Frances Stuart's own version of the facts—The Richmond marriage occasions the fall of Clarendon—His unpopularity and the intrigues against him—The King suspects Lord Cornbury of complicity in the elopement—Clarendon's letter to the King—Fall of Clarendon. 100

CHAPTER VI

Frances missed by the Court—Lord St. Alban's letter to the Duke—Charles refuses his forgiveness—The Duke and Duchess at Cobham Hall—Rumour that an heir is expected—The Duke called away to Dorset—Frances writes to him from Cobham—Peace with Holland—Frances Stuart as Britannia on the Medals—Waller's poem—Madame intercedes for Frances—

CONTENTS

Page

The King rejects her overtures—The Richmonds contemplate retiring to France—Letter from Henry Coventry—Frances at Somerset House—Possibility of a reconciliation discussed—The King holds back—Frances ill with smallpox—Charles hesitates no longer—Lady Castlemaine set by—The King climbs over a garden-gate—Frances appointed a Lady of the Bed-chamber—The Duke and Duchess of Richmond move to Whitehall—Pepys makes the Duke's acquaintance, but fails to meet the Duchess. 131

CHAPTER VII

Scandalous rumours—The Duchess's affection for her husband—Lord Mulgrave's 'Elegy'—The Court at Newmarket—Louis XIV sends over the Abbé Pregnani—His ill-success—The state of the Duke of Richmond's finances—His journey to France—Frances looks after his affairs—Lord Bath's letter—Frances quarrels with Jermyn—Ashley's schemes for the Duke—They come to nothing—Louis XIV proposes to send Madame to England—The difficulties in the way overcome—Madame at Dover—Louise de Keroualle—Death of Madame—Frances at Cobham—Hunting in Charles II's days—Letter from Frances to the Duke—Frances in attendance on the Queen—Their escapade at Audley End—A masked ball—The Queen's ballet—The Court in Norfolk—Charles II's alleged indiscretion at Raynham—The King at Euston—Mock-marriage with Louise de Keroualle—Richmond appointed ambassador to Denmark—Rumours as to the reasons—Why they should be discounted—Rivalry of Frances and Louise de Keroualle . . . 160

CHAPTER VIII

The Duke of Richmond's preparations—He visits the French Ambassador—His arrival in Denmark—His ostentation—Henshaw's position in the embassy—His opinion of the Duke's capacity—Private correspondence of the Duke—His interest in naval and military matters—Walter Stuart—Richmond's dislike for Copenhagen—His letters to his steward at Cobham—Goods sent for from England—Richmond's addiction to drink—His financial affairs entrusted to Frances—His complete faith in her—Francis Digby—Dryden's poem on his death and

CONTENTS

Buckingham's parody—Account of the Duke's death—Arrangements for the funeral—Henshaw appointed ambassador—Charles II's comment on his reluctance—The King's kindness to Frances—The Duke's debts—Petition of the 'Mother of the Maids'—Charles II confers a pension on the Duchess—The Duke's body brought back to England in a Danish ship—The King of Denmark's present to Frances—The Danish Captain rewarded—The Duke's funeral—An elegy written on his death 191

CHAPTER IX

Strained relations between Frances and Lady Catherine O'Brien—Their letters to Lord Essex—Frances sells her life-interest in Cobham Hall—Rumour that she is married to Lord Mulgrave—The Northumberland claimant in the House of Lords—The Duchess of Richmond's finances—The affair of Jack How—Triumphant vindication of the Duchess of Richmond's virtue—Charles II's friendship with Frances—Her skill in dancing—Her fondness for the theatre—Nathaniel Lee—Frances and her cousin, Lord Blantyre—Letter to him—Death of Charles II—More letters to Blantyre. . . 216

CHAPTER X

The Duchess of Richmond's deposition on the birth of the Prince of Wales—Fireworks in St. James's Park—The Revolution—Frances withdraws from Society—Her ill-health—Her pension no longer paid—Petitions to William III and Queen Anne—Her affairs in Scotland entrusted to Blantyre—Her correspondence with him—Her death—The Richmond tomb—The waxen effigy—Frances leaves a considerable fortune—The 'Cat' legend exploded—Minor bequests—The legacy of Lennoxlove—Sale of her pictures and jewels—Purchase of estates in Scotland—Lennoxlove Frances Stuart's real monument—Relics of her there—Her watch—Conclusion . . 238

APPENDIX

The Portraits of La Belle Stuart 260

Index 271

LIST OF ILLUSTRATIONS

		Page
I	La Belle Stuart Frances Stuart as Diana, from the portrait by Sir Peter Lely in the collection of H.M. the King at Hampton Court Palace	*frontispiece*
II	Hampton Court Palace the old East front before Wren's alterations, from the original drawing by Abraham Heckel in the possession of the author	14
III	Charles II from a contemporary engraving	32
IV	Catherine of Bragança from the portrait by S. Verelst at the National Portrait Gallery	64
V	'Mrs Stewart in a buff doublet like a soldier' from an engraving by C. Rivers of the portrait by Jacob Huysman in the collection of H.M. the King at Buckingham Palace	76
VI	Frances Stuart as Pallas from the portrait by H. Gascar in the collection of the Duke of Richmond and Gordon, K.G., at Goodwood House	106
VII	Cobham Hall, Kent from an engraving	134

LIST OF ILLUSTRATIONS

		Page
VIII	Medals by Jan Roettier	
	Fig. 1. The Duchess of Richmond	
	Fig. 2. Obverse of a Peace of Breda medal, 1667	
	Fig. 3. Reverse of Fig. 2. The Duchess of Richmond as Britannia	
	Fig. 4. The Duchess of Richmond	
	Fig. 5. Rejected design for obverse of a Naval Victories Medal	144
IX	Madame Henriette-Anne d'Angleterre, Duchesse d'Orleans	174
X	Charles Stuart, Duke of Richmond and Lennox from the portrait by Sir Peter Lely in the collection of Major W. A. Baird at Lennoxlove	196
XI	Lord Mulgrave from the engraving by George Vertue after a portrait by Sir Godfrey Kneller, prefixed to the 'Works' of John Sheffield, Earl of Mulgrave, Marquess of Normanby, and Duke of Buckingham	220
XII	Frances Teresa Stuart, Duchess of Richmond and Lennox from the portrait by W. Wissing and J. van der Vaart (1687) in the collection of Major W. A. Baird at Lennoxlove	254

CHAPTER I

Restoration of Charles II—Return of the exiled Royalists—Frances Stuart's birth and parentage—Her upbringing at the Queen-Mother's Court—Princess Henrietta married to the Duke of Orleans—Projects for the marriage of Charles II—The Infanta of Portugal chosen—Frances appointed a Maid of Honour—Madame's letter introducing her to Charles II—Arrival of Catherine of Bragança—Marriage of the King—The honeymoon at Hampton Court—The Queen's household—Charles appoints Lady Castlemaine a Lady of the Bed-chamber—His quarrel with the Queen—Clarendon's intervention—Catherine's reconciliation with Lady Castlemaine—Peace at Court.

When the royal vagabond, Charles Stuart, returned after twelve long years of wandering to be restored to the throne of his fathers and joyfully acclaimed by his people as Charles the Second, by the Grace of God, King of Great Britain, France, and Ireland, a new spirit of gaiety entered into his kingdom with him. During the dreary years of the Puritan domination mirth had been banished from these islands, and now mirth was coming back again—with His Majesty as mountebank in chief. Amid the frenzied shouts of the populace, the ringing of bells, and the blare of trumpets, the first comedian of Europe rode into his capital along streets strewn with flowers. All London went on holiday to celebrate his coming: bonfires were lighted; fountains ran with wine as in the fairy-tales; the theatres were reopened, and sounds of music and merriment were to be heard on every side. The King made it abundantly clear that after the bitter years he had passed through he intended to enjoy himself now, and the same spirit was observable in the throng of gay companions which surrounded him. It is true that in the varied crowd of his followers there were many grave and serious-minded men of statesman-like outlook and sincere patriotism, but there were more who were mere triflers careless of anything else but the pleasure of the moment. At intervals during the years that followed the Restoration, Royalist refugees streamed back to England from all corners of Europe, noble gentlemen, who had bravely fought for the father and loyally stood by the son during his years of exile, soldiers of fortune, who had placed their swords at the service of some foreign monarch in his wars, needy and self-seeking adventurers disgorged by the taverns and brothels of France and the Low Countries, where they had whiled away the years of the Commonwealth, roistering, gambling, and wenching. And now they were returning, the virtuous and the vicious, the honest and the dishonest, the wise and the ignorant; the worthier ones to help unselfishly in the re-constitution of the monarchy, the less worthy to join in the eager competition for royal favour. Yet for one brief moment the same sentiment must have animated each one of them from the King downwards —the thrill of homecoming, a feeling that seems to have an intenser and more distinct quality for island-dwellers than for any others.

There were some, however, amongst them, who were to behold their own country for the first time. These were the children, who had been born in exile or carried across the sea when they were too young to be aware of it. Among these last was a young girl, who, early in the year 1662, first looked with conscious eyes on the land from which the fortune of war had driven her soon after her birth. She had been born during the later years of the great Civil War,[1] of a noble Scottish family, which had considered itself bound, not only by feelings of loyalty, but also by ties of blood, to stake its all in defence of the royal House of Stuart. Though boasting only a distant collateral connection, the Blantyres were Stuarts, which means much in a country like Scotland where the clan and family spirit is so strong. With the final defeat of the King's party the position of his more ardent supporters became extremely precarious, and, though Lord Blantyre himself, in spite of his having been one of the 'Engagers,'[2] escaped punishment at the hands

---

[1] Either in 1647 or 1648, more probably the latter.
[2] By the 'Engagement' (December 26th, 1647) the Scots undertook to restore the King by force of arms on condition of his consenting to the establishment of Presbyterianism for a period of three years.

of the victors owing to his youth, his uncle, the Honourable Walter Stuart, M.D., 3rd son of the 1st Lord Blantyre, deemed it wisest to seek shelter abroad. In 1649, a year or so after the birth of his eldest daughter, Frances Teresa, he was able to escape with his family to France and take refuge at the Court of Queen Henrietta Maria.

Save for the fact that he was a doctor, scarcely any details are known of the career of Walter Stuart. He does not appear to have taken his degree in any Scottish or English University, and it seems probable that he gained his medical knowledge at some foreign University, such as Paris or Padua. His wife is as elusive. The only definite facts ascertainable about her are that her Christian name was Sophia, that she had three children, Frances, Sophia, and Walter, and that she was a favoured friend of the Queen-Mother, Henrietta Maria.

It was at the impoverished Court of the widowed Queen that Frances spent her childhood's days. The influences surrounding her in her earliest years were no doubt excellent, if hardly conducive to gaiety. Henrietta Maria, always devout, had been rendered even more so by the succession of misfortunes that had befallen her, and in consequence she spent most of her time in melancholy retirement at the Chateau of Colombes, with occasional lengthy and dreary visits to the Convent of Chaillot. Frances was brought up in the same austere and simple manner that the Queen had prescribed for her own daughter, the Princess Henrietta. The years which followed were fraught with bitterness and despondency for her elders; but the child was yet too young to understand the meaning of the difficulties and disappointments which beset the Royalist Party. The young Prince's expedition to Scotland, his disastrous campaign culminating in the defeat at Worcester, his perilous wanderings as a fugitive in the southern Counties of that kingdom which was rightfully his own, his hard struggles against poverty and prejudice in Germany and Holland: all these events which the exiled Court watched with strained eyes and anxious hearts can have meant little to her. But she was older when the glad news was brought of the death of the usurper Cromwell, and the revival of the monarchy became a possibility. So too when, after a period of anxious doubts, His Majesty's happy Restoration came at last, the changes which it wrought even in her own surroundings cannot have escaped her notice. Hitherto, Henrietta Maria, though herself a daughter of Henry the Great, had been looked on askance by the Court of France, to whom her presence was in fact something of an embarrassment; since Cardinal Mazarin, considering the friendship of England important to France, had brought himself to treat with the government of the usurper. Now, however, the power of Cromwell was no more, and the former exile, shunned by every

Court in Europe, was seated on the throne of England.

The changed attitude of France towards Charles was reflected in the respect suddenly displayed towards his mother, whose presence-chamber was now as thronged as it had formerly been neglected. Moreover, a year or so later, the ties between the two kingdoms were drawn closer by the marriage of the Princess Henrietta, the beloved sister of Charles the Second, to Monsieur, the Duke of Orleans, only brother to the King of France. The alliance was arranged because of the political advantages that would accrue to both royal houses, though as usual the polite fiction was spread abroad that it was a love-match. Monsieur, indeed, endeavoured to give some colour to the pretence by acting the part of a passionate lover with more fervour than felicity, but he did not succeed in convincing even himself, and abandoned the pose at the end of a fortnight. Henrietta never made any serious pretence of being in love with him. He was scarcely a likely object for a woman's love ; for he himself always seemed to have mistaken his sex. He was ridiculously effeminate and cared for nothing in the world but himself, his clothes, and his unworthy favourite, the Chevalier de Lorraine. Yet Henrietta was content enough to be married to him, since all that she desired was to live at the Court of the France which, in spite of the neglect and poverty she had undergone there during the years of exile, she loved so much better than her own country. Had Monsieur been content to let her alone, his contemptible character and unmanly habits would not have perturbed her, but he was soon, at the instigation of his loathsome favourite, to develop a jealous and malicious humour which turned her married life into a misery.

In the 17th century royal marriages were still a most important factor in international politics. It is no wonder therefore that the whole of Europe was eager to know upon whom the new King of England would fix his choice, and that all who hoped to derive any political or personal benefit from the marriage hastened to advance the claims of their own candidate. The views of the Earl of Clarendon, the King's chief adviser, who favoured an alliance with a Protestant princess, for once coincided with those of the greater part of the English people. But a Protestant bride was difficult to find. The daughter of the Dowager Princess of Orange was suggested; but here an insuperable obstacle arose, for Charles as King refused point-blank to marry a lady by whom his addresses as a penniless exile had been scornfully rejected. The partizans of a Protestant marriage could find no other ladies of suitable age and rank save in Germany; but on the subject of an alliance with a German Princess His Majesty shared the views of King Henry VIII., and his remarks on the unprepossessing appearance of Teutonic damsels were as forcible and plain-spoken as the opinion expressed by the Tudor monarch on the charms of the unfortunate Anne of Cleves. It seemed inevitable therefore that a bride must be chosen from the Roman Catholic princesses of Portugal, Spain, or Italy. The claims of the Infanta of Portugal were assiduously advanced by Louis XIV. who was anxious to provide an ally for Portugal in her struggle with Spain, now that the Treaty of the Pyrenees and his own marriage with a Spanish princess debarred him from himself affording overt assistance. The portrait of the Infanta was sent to Charles, who professed himself delighted with her appearance, a fact which is sufficiently surprising, if the portrait he was shown was really, as Horace Walpole asserts, that curious picture by Dirk Stoop in his own collection at Strawberry Hill.[1] His estimate of her beauty may, however, have been considerably influenced by the recital of her proposed dowry, which, in addition to a large sum of money, was to give him Bombay, Tangier, and trading privileges in the Portuguese possessions. Hard cash was always acceptable to Charles the Second, and it was thought that the other concessions might reconcile his people to a Roman Catholic marriage; for, as the King himself once wisely

[1] It is now in the National Portrait Gallery.

noted, " the thing which is nearest the harte of the nation is trade and all that belongs to it."[1] A committee of Privy Councillors to whom Charles referred the proposals of the Portuguese envoy unanimously declared that, if he were bound to embark upon a Catholic alliance, the Portuguese marriage would without doubt be the most advantageous, and after this the question seemed to be practically decided, though everything was nearly upset at the last moment by the Earl of Bristol, who, at the instigation of Spain, actually prevailed upon the King to entertain the project of an Italian marriage. Fortunately His Majesty's more honourable advisers pointed out to him that he had by now gone too far with the Portuguese negotiations to recede, and Bristol's plans collapsed. It was not long before all the world knew that the daughter of the House of Bragança was to be the Queen-Consort of England.

The necessity of forming a household for the new Queen caused a flutter in the hearts of all who might hope to be chosen for a place in it The King's tastes were already so notorious that it was obvious there would be no place for dulness and melancholy in the Court of England. Youth and gaiety would triumph there, and a capacity for enjoying life would be the surest path to royal favour. Little Frances Stuart was among the first to be singled out for the

---

[1] Charles II to Madame. September 14th, 1668.

honour of serving the future Queen. This was due not only to her high birth and to a desire to recompense the loyal services of her family, but also to her own charm and beauty. Though only fourteen or at most fifteen years of age, she had already become a great favourite with the Queen-Mother and her Court, and was the petted darling of the lively young Duchess of Orleans. Her appointment pleased everyone, or almost everyone, for there was one personage who did his utmost to keep her in France. This was the young king himself, who had already noticed her growing beauty and assured her mother that, if she were allowed to remain in France, he would himself provide her with a dowry and arrange an illustrious marriage for her. It has even been asserted that he declared that he ' loved her not as a mistress, but as one that he could marry as well as any lady in France.' But Mrs. Stuart with great wisdom refused to take seriously protestations that were probably not meant seriously, and was not to be diverted from her intentions regarding her daughter's future. Foiled in his endeavours, the King accepted her refusal with a good grace and presented the object of his admiration with a valuable jewel as a parting-gift. Her mother had taken care to provide herself with something almost if not quite as valuable in a letter of introduction to Charles II. from the Duchess of Orleans, since it was certain that the favour of the King would readily be extended to anyone recommended to him by his dearest Minette, as he was wont to call this favourite sister. Moreover, the terms in which Henrietta described the girl were well calculated to arouse the interest of so fervent an admirer of feminine beauty

January the 4th.[1]

"I did not wish to lose this opportunity of writing to you by Madame Stuart, who is taking her daughter to be one of the maids of the Queen, your wife. If it had not been for such a purpose, I can assure you that I should have been very sorry to let her go from here, for she is the prettiest girl in the world and the most fitted to adorn a court. Yesterday I received a letter in reply to the one I sent you by Crofts,[2] and no one could be more pleased than I am at the very thought of being able to see Your Majesty once again: in truth, this is the thing in the world I wish for most, and that you would believe me your most humble servant."

Catherine of Bragança did not arrive in England till May. In accordance with the terms of the marriage treaty a brave fleet, under the Earl of

---

[1] The original of this letter is in French and is to be found at Lambeth Palace (Cod. Tenison 645 p. 48), with several others from Henriette to Charles. It is unfortunate that, while a large number of his letters to her are in existence, (in the Ministère des Affaires Etrangères in Paris,) so few of hers should be discoverable. This particular letter, which bears no year-date, is often wrongly attributed to the year 1663; it is, however, quite obviously her reply to Charles's letter dated 16th December, 1661.

[2] William, Lord Crofts.

Sandwich, had been sent out early in the year to take possession of Tangier and to bring the bride back from Lisbon on its return journey. But certain difficulties had supervened and entailed delay. Sandwich was detained for some time in Tangier. He had apprehended that he would have some difficulty in obtaining possession of the town; since public feeling in Portugal was strongly against the surrender of so important a post into the hands of heretics, and it was considered likely that the Governor would refuse to obey the orders of the Queen-Regent. But if such an intention was harboured it could not be carried out; for a few days before the arrival of the English fleet the Portuguese garrison had sallied forth and suffered so annihilating a defeat at the hands of the Moors that the town was left almost entirely unprotected. Lord Sandwich was obliged to provide the place with a temporary garrison and remain there until the new Governor, Lord Peterborough, arrived with his troops. Neither did Sandwich find his task any too simple when he reached Lisbon. The fear of a Spanish invasion had caused the Queen-Regent to draw upon a great part of the Infanta's dowry, and the unfortunate English Admiral was called upon to decide whether or not he ought to accept the Princess unless the exact provisions of the marriage-contract were fulfilled. In the end he decided to do so, especially as he had already taken possession of Tangier. On his own responsibility he made provisional arrangements for the payment of the remainder of the dowry. At last everything was satisfactorily settled, and the fleet bearing the King's bride on board set sail for England and after a stormy but otherwise uneventful voyage came into harbour at Portsmouth.

As the Portuguese Infanta was still suffering from the effects of the voyage, she can hardly have been displeased at heart to learn that Parliamentary business had detained the King in London. But with his accustomed gallantry His Majesty hastened to prove that his belated arrival was not due to indifference ; for he made the journey to Portsmouth with the greatest speed that the communications of those times would allow, and, pausing only to exchange his dusty garments for others more suited to the occasion, he eagerly waited upon his future bride in her bed-chamber. On the next day took place the marriage ceremony, at which the Bishop of London officiated. Another service according to the Roman Catholic rites was conducted in private by the Queen's Almoner, Aubigny.

Although Charles is reported to have confided to one of his libertine friends that his wife resembled nothing more than a bat, to Clarendon he wrote professing himself extremely pleased with her. She was not exactly beautiful, he told the Chancellor, but she had lovely eyes, a most agreeable voice, and so sweet an expression that he was sure they would be great friends. It must be confessed that others were not so enthusiastic in their praises. The standard of beauty required of princesses need not be very high, since the glamour of their position in itself obscures so many deficiencies, but contemporary accounts are far from panegyrical, though it is obvious that all did their best to emphasize her more comely features, and discriminating critics gave ungrudging praise to her lustrous and languishing eyes. But no one felt obliged to extend such indulgence towards her following of Portuguese ladies, and on this subject more outspoken comments were made. Ugly and ill-favoured in their persons, their appearance was rendered still more grotesque by the monstrous old-fashioned farthingales or 'guardinfantas' with which they accentuated rather than concealed their defects. They must, indeed, have formed a curious contrast in silhouette with those ladies of Catherine's English household who awaited her at Portsmouth.

For the honeymoon the King's choice had fallen upon Hampton Court Palace, because it was accounted not only the stateliest and most luxurious of the royal residences out of London, but also that in the healthiest situation. It was at this time a curious irregular pile of red brick: its numerous slender turrets with their cupolas surmounted by gilded weather-vanes forming a jagged outline against the sky and giving it the semblance of some

HAMPTON COURT PALACE: THE OLD EAST FRONT
Abraham Heckel

fantastic fairy-city. The Royal progress thither was stately but slow. The King and Queen travelled in a superb chariot drawn by six horses, and a long procession of carriages followed after. The foremost of these contained the ladies and officers of the royal household, the remainder the servants and baggage. Charles laughingly maintained that one waggon was exclusively devoted to the vast farthingales of his wife's Portuguese ladies. A night was spent at Windsor Castle on the way, and towards evening on May 29th, His Majesty's birthday, Hampton Court Palace was reached. Catherine was now attended by ladies of both nationalities, though the English attendants were as yet few, for even now her household had not been finally settled. On the 10th of June Lord Cornbury wrote to the Marchioness of Worcester : ' We have yett[1] a very unsettled family, nothing at all in order. Not one Lady of the Bed-chamber named beside my Lady Suffolke who is in wayting, and they say both the number and persons you formerly heard mentioned will be very much altered. The four dressers are fixed, who are my Lady Wood, Lady Scroope, Mrs. Fraizer, Mrs. La Garde. The Mayds of Honour are likewise in wayting, viz., Mrs. Cary, Mrs.[2] Stuart, Mrs. Wells Mrs. Price, Mrs. Boynton, Mrs. Warmestry.'

[1] Hist. MSS. Comm. Report. Beaufort MSS., p. 53.

[2] ' Mrs ' was the usual appellation for an unmarried lady at this period, the term ' Miss ' having an uncomplimentary significance.

The King himself soon determined to remedy the deficiency in the number of Ladies of the Bedchamber by appointing to that post his mistress, Barbara Villiers, Countess of Castlemaine, the unworthy daughter of one of the noblest of Cavaliers, Lord Grandison, who had died of wounds received fighting for Charles I. at Edgehill. Her brilliant beauty had first attracted the attention of the King to her when she was living in Holland as an exile with her young husband, Roger Palmer. The King had thought fit to repay the loyal services of her family by making her his mistress, and Barbara had been nothing loth to put a free interpretation on her family tradition of loyalty to the monarch. The connection had endured after the King was restored to his throne, indeed so infatuated had he become that he spent with her the night of his return to his capital. At such a time it might have been imagined that his heart and mind would have been occupied with other things, but with Charles, as ever, love conquered everything.

It was a fit inauguration of his reign. Henceforth Mistress Palmer held undisputed sway over his heart and purse in spite of the disapproval of the powerful Chancellor, who carried his objections to her so far as to refuse categorically to affix the Great Seal to any grants made to her by the King. Charles the Second's method of dealing with the situation was characteristic of him. Determined upon conferring a title on his mistress's unwilling husband, he was yet reluctant to offend Clarendon's moral scruples and accordingly created Roger Palmer Earl of Castlemaine in the Kingdom of Ireland, where the Chancellor's moral standard was evidently less rigid.

It was generally supposed that the dismissal of the 'Lady,' as she was nicknamed by the courtiers, would be an inevitable consequence of the King's marriage; but Lady Castlemaine herself chose to think otherwise, and showed that she had no intention of retiring into the background. The fact that the King had already acknowledged the parentage of one of her children constituted in her eyes a confirmation of her claim to be 'maitresse en titre,' and she saw no reason why the King's marriage should upset this arrangement. She was again expecting a child by the King, and openly declared her determination to lie in at Hampton Court. Her brazen effrontery served her well, for she knew that though Charles might have consented to her effacing herself of her own accord, he would never bring himself to consent to her expulsion from Court. But his decision to place her in his wife's household was wholly unexpected and therefore caused much consternation among the more decent-minded and a joyful excitement among the ribald, who saw the prospect of an entertaining situation. It is always hard to unravel the complicated workings of Charles the Second's peculiar mind, but in this instance his motives are more than ever inexplicable. If he still intended to continue his intimacy with Lady Castlemaine, his action was both brutal and foolish, and Charles was in general neither a brute nor a fool. On this occasion he apparently lost himself in a maze of subtleties and actually succeeded in deceiving himself when he protested that, if Lady Castlemaine were placed in constant association with his wife, he would be subjected to less temptation or at least gifted with fewer opportunities of renewing the old relations; moreover, as he thought, it was only just that the highest possible honour should be her recompense for the loss of his favours. Preposterous as his arguments may be, there seems to be no reason for doubting the King's sincerity in these professions. But, whether his intention sprang from good or bad motives, there can be no doubt that it was a serious breach of the simplest rules of tact and good taste. Catherine, who had promised her mother that she would never even allow Lady Castlemaine's name to be mentioned in her presence, could scarcely comprehend that an indignity of still greater magnitude was contemplated. Far less could she be expected to fathom the subtleties of her husband's reasoning. The narrow atmosphere of the convent in which she had been brought up was scarcely calculated to teach her to appreciate the bewildering sophistries of a Court. Her moral sense shocked, her dignity outraged, she utterly refused to admit Lady Castlemaine into her presence. The King expostulated; the Queen remained obdurate; and the Court for the most part sided with the King, as the Queen's quiet disposition and distaste for the boisterous gaiety which characterized the Court had already contributed to render her unpopular. The King at last stooped to an infamous trick. Trading upon his wife's ignorance of the English language and consequent inability to realize until too late what was happening, he one evening succeeded in introducing Lady Castlemaine into her presence-chamber. Catherine, not dreaming who she was, rose and received her with her usual graciousness. A moment later the subdued titters and meaning glances of the bystanders showed her that her husband was actually flaunting her rival in her face. Overwhelmed with shame she fell back in her seat; her colour came and went as she endeavoured to restrain her tears; but all in vain, for they would fall. Then, mercifully for her, she fainted and was carried away into her private apartments.

Was Charles at last ashamed of himself? Certainly he showed during the next few days that he was disconcerted and ill-at-ease, and appeared half-inclined to abandon his project, especially as most of the right-minded people at the Court supported the Queen, and even his adored sister, Henriette, to whom he had complained of Catherine's conduct, felt obliged to tell him that she thought his wife had good cause for offence. But certain among the younger courtiers were determined not to allow him to recede and represented to him that to yield now would be a sign of weakness, and would give all the world the impression that he was governed by his wife. They told him that princes ought to have liberties which private men had not, that he was entitled to keep a mistress, and ought to assert himself on this point at the outset of his married life. Fortified by their insidious persuasions, he re-entered the unequal struggle with added vigour and even went to the length of calling upon the Chancellor to remonstrate with the Queen.

To Clarendon, who loathed Lady Castlemaine, such a task was eminently distasteful, and it was at best an ignoble part that he was called upon to play, for how could he in honesty persuade the Queen to accept in her own household a woman whom he deemed so infamous that he had forbidden his own wife to receive her? He did, indeed, attempt to point out to the King that it was both hard-hearted and cruel to make a request to the Queen, 'which flesh and blood could not comply with,' and represented also the injury it would do to his reputation among his people. But Charles only replied that he was bound both in conscience and honour to recompense Lady Castlemaine for the wrong he had done her, and maintained that his relations with her would henceforth be innocent. Seeing that the King was not to be moved from his resolution, Clarendon readjusted his own notions of 'conscience and honour,' and consented to approach the Queen. He speedily withdrew, however, when he found he could get nothing from her but tears. On the following day he made another attempt, but again without any success. The King and Queen alternately quarrelled and sulked while Clarendon continued his efforts, which he was at last forced to abandon in despair. A deadlock had been reached, and for some days the Queen sat by miserable and neglected, while the King devoted himself entirely to the society of his boon-companions. But Clarendon's persuasions had made more impression on her than she had at first been willing to own; one day her attitude suddenly changed, and of her own accord, when nobody was expecting it, she called Lady Castlemaine to her and spoke to her in friendly fashion. It was an ill-timed surrender, if she had only known it. The King's gaiety was all a pretence; he was rapidly growing tired of the sordid quarrel, and if she had only held out a little longer, she might have had her own way. Her spirited refusal to yield to persuasions and threats had won Charles's grudging admiration, and he was seriously thinking of begging her forgiveness. But her sudden weakness at the moment when he had begun to love her for her firmness filled him with annoyance and disappointment. He was even unkinder to her now than he had been before, and extended his displeasure towards those who adhered to her. They were few enough in all conscience; since Charles had become imbued with the perfectly just notion that her opposition to him had been encouraged by her Portuguese followers, and had consequently obliged her to dismiss most of them.[1]

Generally ignored even in her own apartments, while a throng of eager flatterers surrounded the imperious favourite, who flaunted herself in her presence like a peacock, the unfortunate Queen found her life a sad and dreary one. But she was a woman of great good sense, and, when courage returned to her again, she determined to make the best of a situation from which she realized that she could not escape. While she still treated Lady Castlemaine with studied politeness and sought her society instead of shunning it, she resolved to stifle the indignation she felt for her husband and to do everything she could to please him with her gentleness and consideration. By these means the atmosphere of the Court became outwardly tranquil, and, though the Castlemaine's triumph was ostensibly assured, and her position as titular mistress tacitly acknowledged, the King was only too eager to show that he appreciated Catherine's generosity, with the result that between husband and wife there arose a placid

[1] Clarendon. Continuation 358-392.

and enduring affection which made the Lady's actual influence much less than it seemed. In many little ways the Queen endeavoured to show her affection for her husband. When he went to London for the day to attend a Council, she would go out part of the way with her ladies to meet him on his return in the evening. Such attentions delighted him, and he openly expressed his pleasure. And so all the trouble between them was at an end when the Queen-Mother came over from France to see her son's wife. Visits were exchanged between Hampton Court and Greenwich, where Henrietta Maria was staying while Somerset House was being prepared for her. Avowedly delighted that Charles had chosen a Catholic bride, Henrietta Maria was predisposed to approve of Catherine and was not disappointed. At least the Queen could always count on a firm ally in her mother-in-law.

And now peace reigned in Wolsey's old red palace by the water, and the Court devoted itself wholeheartedly to its usual occupation of extracting all the enjoyment possible out of life. Cupid, who finds work for idle hearts to do, shot many arrows with devastating effect as King Charles the Second's Courtiers wandered among the lime trees in the Park, or in the gardens, along the famous cradle walk of wych-elm and the parterre known by the romantic name of 'Paradise.'

CHAPTER II

Royal entry into London—Frances Stuart's friendship with Lady Castlemaine—The King falls in love with her—Gramont's opinion of Frances—Her beauty—The story of the green stockings—Arrival of Cominges—His contempt for the English Court—Charles II. and Frances—Report of a mock-marriage—The Duke of Monmouth's wedding—The Court Ball—The Marquis de Ruvigny—Lady Castlemaine's quarrel with Frances and its settlement—The Queen and her ladies riding in the Park.

At the end of August (1662) their Majesties made their state entry into their capital, which the King had commanded his lieges to have swept and garnished against the coming of their Queen. The journey from Hampton Court Palace was made by water, and the broadness of the river gave the loyal citizens of London the fullest opportunities to arrange an elaborate welcome. The barges of the City Companies were disguised as floating islands from which river-deities apostrophized their Majesties in verse. Everyone who could by hook or by crook procure a vessel of any sort came out to greet the King and Queen, and it is said that there were so many boats on the river that day that the water was scarcely visible. And thus the imposing procession swept down the river to Westminster amid the strains of music that, since they were produced by many different orchestras which could scarcely have been playing the same air, were perhaps fortunately drowned by the peal of ordnance and the cheering of the people who crowded the banks. When the stately open vessel, rowed by twenty-four bargemen in brilliant scarlet liveries, came into view, the cheering grew louder and more enthusiastic, for here were the King and Queen seated beneath a canopy of cloth of gold supported by Corinthian pillars gracefully festooned with flowers. The thirst of the people for glittering pageantry was not yet sated, and it was by demonstrations such as these that they expressed their relief at the disappearance of the Puritans' drab rule.

With the Court at Whitehall the peaceful settlement achieved by Catherine's good sense still endured. Lady Castlemaine took up her place in the Queen's household without further opposition. Catherine's apparent friendliness with Lady Castlemaine must serve as Frances Stuart's justification for the affection which now sprang up between her and the royal mistress. Loyalty to the Queen, whose Maid of Honour she was, should, it is true, have forbidden her to seek the friendship of her rival; but an inexperienced child fresh from the devout and virtuous Court of Henrietta Maria could scarcely be expected to appreciate the true state of affairs and to realize that bitter enmity lay concealed beneath the outward mask of friendliness. The brilliant beauty of the Lady would easily captivate a child, who could not see the evil that was in her. What is far more difficult to understand is Lady Castlemaine's reason for deliberately attracting the King's notice to Frances Stuart. The girl was present at every entertainment she gave for the King, and very often she kept her to sleep, so that the King, who usually visited her in the morning before she rose, often found Frances in bed with her. Perhaps the beautiful Barbara, confident in her own superlative charms did not apprehend that any danger could arise from a girl of fourteen or fifteen, or perhaps, as Gramont suggests, she actually encouraged His Majesty to make love to Frances in the hope of distracting his attention from the intrigue she was at that time conducting with young Jermyn, nephew of the Queen-Mother's reputed husband, the Earl of St. Alban's. Lady Castlemaine was far from being faithful to her royal lover. Throughout her long connection with him she indulged in an unending succession of intrigues with other men. It is true that she did not expect constancy from him either; on the whole she was disposed to be indulgent towards his affairs with other women, fearing only such rivals as could move him to generosity as well as love and thus deprive her of some of the perquisites of her place. Frances Stuart, she thought, was too young and too frivolous to know how to use her opportunities, and it was far better that the King should dally for a time with her than that he should fix his attentions on some more dangerous rival, who would not be so easy to dislodge.

Lady Castlemaine was soon to discover that she had made a miscalculation. That Charles should fall a speedy victim to Frances Stuart's beauty was only to be expected and gave her no cause for alarm, since it was well known that there was no beauty so exquisite that it would not pall on the King sooner or later ; but Frances possessed a gift more dangerous than her beauty in a sense of humour. She laughed at the King's jokes and won his heart. Although she possessed no extraordinary wit herself, she appreciated the gift in others, and nothing could delight Charles more, since a ready listener was far more attractive to him than a brilliant talker. Bored with politics and depressed by the greedy ambition and sordid intrigues of those who surrounded him, he was irresistibly drawn towards Frances by her good nature and unaffected gaiety. He was rejoiced to find in her a dislike as acute as his own for the serious things of life, a failing which, it must be admitted, was far more excusable in a child of her age than in a man of His Majesty's maturer years. The Chevalier de Gramont, however, was not disposed to make any allowances for her youth. His contempt for her was profound. "It is hardly possible for a woman to have less wit or more beauty," is his considered estimate of Frances Stuart. " She was childish in her behaviour and laughed at everything, and her taste for frivolous amusements, though unaffected, was only allowable in a girl of about twelve or thirteen years old. A child, however, she was in every other respect, except playing with a doll ; Blind-man's buff was her most favourite amusement ; she was building castles of cards, while the deepest play was going on in her apartments, where you saw her surrounded by eager courtiers, who handed her the cards, or young architects, who endeavoured to imitate her."[1]

Pursuits such as these must have been exceedingly irritating to Gramont, who literally lived on the proceeds of his card-playing. It is, indeed, not uncharitable to suggest that his contempt for Frances had its origin in her ability to divert the attention of the company from serious gambling. The wherewithal to support a gentleman at the Court of England was not to be obtained by indulging in blind-man's buff or any other of the frivolous amusements which Frances brought into fashion. The King, on the other hand, was delighted, for gambling offered no real attractions to him. It is said that he himself rarely risked as much as five pounds at play, and disliked to see ladies playing at all,[2] though his

[1] Memoirs of Chevalier de Gramont.

[2] John Sheffield, Duke of Buckingham. "A character of Charles II, King of England."

opinions on this point were, of course, entirely disregarded by most of the fair ladies who graced his Court.

While Frances Stuart's gaiety and charm made her enchanting to the King as a companion, his senses were held in thrall by her peerless beauty. Golden-brown hair in which red lights glinted here and there crowned the small head poised on a neck that had the smoothness and clarity of alabaster. She possessed a bewitching nose, eyes like harebells, and an exquisite mouth, the upper lip rivalling the curve of the bow which Lely has placed in her hand in his most famous portrait of her, the lower rather full, a little petulant, and perilously fascinating. Though tall and straight, she was slender and very graceful. It was in this grace which accompanied her every movement that her chiefest charm consisted, for, beautiful as she was, she had no desire to be a cold, proud goddess set motionless on a pinnacle to be worshipped from afar. The feathery lightness with which she danced, the peculiar grace with which she sat her horse seemed to enhance her beauty and add to it a radiance that was lacking when she was in repose. Beauty, if adorned at all, must be adorned with good taste, and this she did not lack; for, as De Gramont says with justifiable partiality for his own country, " she possessed in perfection that air of dress which is so much admired, and which cannot be attained, unless it is taken when young in France."

Connoisseurs are perhaps right in believing that when anything is well nigh perfect it is worth while discovering its faults, and critics were not lacking to decry the beauty of Frances Stuart. Gramont asserted that her appearance was more showy than engaging,[1] and also criticized her figure in a sentence which somehow seems to contradict itself, declaring that "her shape was not good, though she was slender, straight enough, and taller than the generality of women," while others proclaimed that her figure would have been faultless had her waist been less high and her carriage less stiff. But whatever strictures were made on her figure, there seems to have been nothing save admiration for the shapeliness of her legs, which throughout her life drew forth rapturous comments from privileged observers. A trifling incident at this time showed in what repute they were held. The winter of 1662 was exceedingly severe; in December the snow lay thick on the ground, the Thames was frozen over, and on the water in St. James's Park the Court created much interest by skating, an accomplishment acquired in Holland during the years of exile and hitherto unknown in England. Such weather was by no means inappropriate for the arrival of an imposing and befurred embassy from the Tzar of Muscovy. The King received the ambassadors on

---

[1] C'était une figure de plus d'éclat qu'elle n'était touchante.

December the 29th and accepted their master's rich presents of furs, hawks, cloths of tissue, Persian carpets, and sea-horse teeth.[1] That evening at Court all the conversation was on the subject of the Russian ambassadors and their outlandish appearance. Somebody remarked that he had heard that Russian women were very handsome and had handsome legs. Whereupon His Majesty, who was in jocular mood, resolutely maintained that no one could have handsomer legs than Frances Stuart. Ingenuousness was one of Frances's chief characteristics, and she was not in the least averse to allowing the company to test the truth of an opinion expressed by so exalted an authority and shared in all candour by herself. She therefore unaffectedly lifted her skirt above the knee that the onlookers might judge for themselves. The King's opinion was promptly and triumphantly vindicated, the Duke of York alone dissenting. He professed himself unable to give unstinted praise to a leg that was so slender; legs, he thought, should be shorter and thicker, and to be quite perfect should be encased in green stockings. The reasons for the Duke's preference were probably hidden from most of those present; but Lord Chesterfield, who had for some time suspected that an intrigue was on foot between the Duke and his wife, felt his worst fears confirmed when he

---

[1] Pepys. Dec. 29th, 1662. Evelyn. Dec. 29th, 1662.

recognized this most accurate description of her Ladyship's legs. And that explains why the Earl and Countess of Chesterfield left for the wilds of Derbyshire in a great hurry the very next day.

About this time there arrived in England a new French ambassador, the Comte de Cominges. It was Louis XIV's object to prevent the possibility of an offensive alliance against France of the two great maritime powers, Holland and England, and to secure the English alliance for himself. The chief stumbling-block to this project was the traditional hatred of the English people for the French. His only hope therefore was to aid Charles in establishing an autocratic government that would make him independent of his people and able to force them into an alliance with France against their inclinations. Charles, who hated the Dutch for their Republican principles, was ready enough to fall in with the French king's schemes, and declared himself willing to make an intimate connection between the two crowns the basis of his foreign policy. But the King of England was, as Louis well knew, as subtle as a serpent and as slippery as an eel, and it was obvious that some method must be found of binding him to his word. Since his besetting weaknesses were extravagance and love of women, Louis soon realized that he could be effectively chained with golden fetters and bound with silken cords. The French Ambassador was instructed to

CHARLES II

keep his finger on the pulse of the English Court and to relate to his master all gossip that he could gather, especially that which concerned the King's amours.

In comparison with the splendid and elegant Court of the Roi Soleil Cominges found the Court of Charles the Second dull and provincial. True, there were plays and dances almost every day, but an attempt to produce one of those magnificent ballets that had delighted him in France was a lamentable failure. Even had the necessary funds for it been available, Cominges still thought it could never have been a success, because there was nobody who knew how to dance, still less how to produce or invent a plot. Gaming was the chief employment of the courtiers, who gathered every day for that purpose in the Queen's apartments, or preferably in those of Lady Castlemaine, who took care to provide a good supper for the players. 'This Sire', concluded Cominges contemptuously, ' is how they pass the time here '.[1] As for love, it seemed to the French Ambassador that in England they scarcely even knew the meaning of the word. Except for a few affairs which were already dragging to a dreary end the English Court seemed to him as innocent from choice as was an assembly of aged women from necessity. Frances Stuart was the only young girl amongst them all, who even thought of conquering men's hearts.[2]

[1] CA 79 Cominges to Louis XIV. Jan. 25th, 1663.
[2] CA 79 Cominges to Louis XIV. Jan. 31st, 1663.

In view of the notorious licentiousness of the English Court, Cominges must be accounted very unobservant, unless it be that his ignorance of the English temperament led him to suppose that love was fading when it was really in full flower. They made love more ostentatiously in France, and the exception he made in favour of Frances Stuart was probably due to the fact that her upbringing in France had made her coquetry of a kind which he was able to recognize.

The King was now beginning to fall deeply and genuinely in love with Frances, and made no attempt to disguise his passion. Considering His Majesty's reputation it is not surprising that most people at once concluded that she had become his mistress. What is more strange is that even in those days some were found to maintain that she had kept her innocence. That any doubt on the subject existed at all in an age when decency was disregarded and vice was openly and shamelessly paraded is in itself sufficiently suggestive. She herself always maintained that she had never surrendered to the King's importunities, and her subsequent actions go far to prove the truth of her assertions, so far indeed that one cannot but conclude that, if she ever was the King's mistress, her whole career was the most consummately consistent network of hypocrisy that was ever devised by the artful mind of woman.

In these early years at least she seems to have

La Belle Stuart

been no more than a wayward butterfly, a child who wanted to be amused and petted and was prepared to obtain what she wanted by smiles and kisses, while all the time her cold little heart was free from the passions and pains of love. There is no doubt that she encouraged the King's advances, but her fault lay not in succumbing to them, but in drawing him on without any intention of satisfying his desires. At the time, of course, many put a different construction upon her conduct. Tales of the manner in which the King had triumphed over her virtue were even freely recounted at Court. Pepys heard a rumour ' how Lady Castlemaine, a few days since, had Mrs. Stuart to an entertainment and at night they begun a frolique that they two must be married—and married they were, with ring and all other ceremonies of church-service, and ribbands and a sack posset in bed, and flinging the stocking; but in the close, it is said that my Lady Castlemaine, who was the bridegroom, rose, and the King come and took her place. This is said to be very true.'[1]

There is no reason to believe that the ' frolique' did not take place, for diversions of this kind were eminently characteristic of the time, and much amusement could be derived from a travesty of the quaint usages that attended the ceremony of bedding the married pair, and tearing up their

---

[1] Pepys. Feb. 8th, 1663.

ribbands and garters to distribute as favours among the guests. Herrick describes these customs in his 'Epithalamia on Sir Clipseby Crew and his Lady':

> 'Quickly, quickly then prepare;
> And let the young men and the brides-maids share
> Your garters; and their joints
> Encircle with the bridegroom's points.
>
> If needs we must for ceremony's sake
> Bless a sack possit; luck go with it; take
> The night-charm quickly;

But it is most unlikely that the joke had the culmination suggested by Pepys. Lady Castlemaine may have originally encouraged the friendship between Charles and Frances, but she was beginning to take alarm now and was not such a fool as to bring about the very thing that would compass her own downfall. She could afford to disregard the King's intrigues with actresses and courtezans; but a mistress of a rank equal to her own would be far too dangerous. Nor had Frances anything to gain by surrendering to the King. It was not as if she craved political influence, or even money and titles like Lady Castlemaine; all that she desired was pleasure and admiration, and of these she had her fill. The King's passion for her was obvious to everyone, and as a consequence she was sought after, and flattered, and spoilt to her heart's content.

On April the 20th of this year there took place the wedding of the King's natural son, the Duke of Monmouth, to Lady Anne Scott, daughter and heiress of the Earl of Buccleuch. The Duke was a mere boy of sixteen, while little Lady Anne was only twelve, so the Court regarded the wedding as just another diverting game. The King himself looked upon the affair as an immense joke. He wrote to the Duchess of Orleans :—' You must not by this post expect a long letter from me, this being Jameses marriage day, and I am going to sup with them, where we intend to dance and see them a bed together, but the ceremony shall stop there, for they are both too young to lye all night together.'[1]

At the ball that evening the glorious beauty of Frances Stuart amazed all comers, and it was universally acknowledged that she was beyond all doubt the fairest lady at the Court of England. The only person who could have rivalled her was Lady Castlemaine; but on this occasion circumstances had placed her at a disadvantage, for she was once more with child—by the King, so she averred, though there were some who whispered that the prodigality with which she dispensed her favours made this claim at least open to question. The superb jewels and magnificent dress she was wearing could not disguise her thinness and pallor, which became more

[1] Charles to Madame. April 20th, 1663.

marked when contrasted with the dazzling beauty of her rival. She herself was the first to be conscious of La Belle Stuart's triumph and displayed her jealousy so openly that Cominges noticed it and wrote to inform Louis that Mademoiselle Stuart, whom His Majesty would remember having seen in France, was causing great uneasiness to a certain lady, and, he added, with the exquisite vision of Frances still fresh in his mind, not without reason.[1]

Lady Castlemaine's influence was now at its lowest ebb. The King still continued to visit her, but he was never now in the same expansive mood as he had used to be in when he was with her, and those of her political friends, who had always counted upon approaching the King in her apartments under favourable conditions, when they designed to frustrate or override the counsels of the Lord Chancellor Clarendon and the Treasurer Southampton, now found him distant in his manner and unwilling to listen to them. The Marquis de Ruvigny, who had recently come over on a special mission from France, was persuaded that Lady Castlemaine was no longer the King's mistress. On June 15th he wrote to Louis: 'No one doubts but that Miss Stuart has taken her place. She did not partake of the Communion at Whitsun, which is an assured mark of their recent understanding, so

[1] CA. 79. Cominges to Louis, April 20th, 1663.

the best Catholics inform me.¹ He sees her as secretly as possible and she is one of the most beautiful and modest girls one could see.'²

This is perhaps the most weighty accusation that has ever been made against Frances Stuart's virtue; but, devout Catholic as she was, it is always conceivable that she may have had other reasons for not taking the Sacrament on this occasion.

Enraged by the King's coldness, Lady Castlemaine had now come to the end of her patience and determined to take action against Frances. She publicly announced that henceforward she would neither invite her nor receive her in her apartments. But, unfortunately for her, the King's affections were now so seriously engaged that he unhesitatingly declared for his part that he would never set foot in Lady Castlemaine's apartments again except when Frances was there.³ The fury of Lady Castlemaine at this defeat passed all bounds; she gathered together all her possessions and departed to her house at Richmond. If Frances had really deliberately displaced the Lady and become the King's mistress in her stead, she could not have failed to rejoice at her departure from the field. She was, on the other hand, most distressed, and, in spite of Charles's

---

[1] Ruvigny himself was a Huguenot.
[2] CA. 80. Ruvigny to Louis XIV, June 15th, 1663.
[3] CA. 80. Cominges to Louis XIV, July 5th, 1663.

utter indifference to what became of Lady Castlemaine, she determined to do her utmost to persuade her to return to Court. She even went so far as to insist upon going herself to see the infuriated Countess and prevailed upon young Berkeley, a great favourite at Court, to accompany her down to Richmond. What happened at that interview nobody ever discovered; but, either Frances was able to convince Lady Castlemaine that she had no desire to take her place, or else Berkeley's arguments were effective; for the Lady finally consented to return to Whitehall and to rescind her decision not to receive Frances.[1]

The King was not so easily disposed to forgive the Lady, since she had committed the unpardonable sin of upsetting his equanimity. On her reappearance he treated her with marked coldness, which, however, was perhaps not wholly due to her recent misbehaviour, for it was believed that the Queen was pregnant, and the hopes of an heir had drawn him closer to her. The solicitude he was now displaying for his wife was universally remarked and applauded. Catherine had become much more popular of late. In spite of the prejudice against her as a foreigner and a Roman Catholic, she had won the people's respectful admiration by her graciousness and gentle nature. Her outlook too had

[1] CA. 80. Various despatches from Cominges and Ruvigny, July 1663.

broadened considerably, and she was beginning to take a lively interest in the diversions of the Court. Pepys saw the King and Queen riding together one day in the Park with the ladies of their Court. Charles and Catherine were riding hand-in-hand, and doubtless the Queen's pleasure at receiving such marks of her husband's affection beautified her; for she looked exceedingly pretty in her riding-dress of white and crimson. The courtiers, following the King's lead, ignored Lady Castlemaine, who was present, wearing a brilliant yellow plume in her hat. No one pressed forward to assist her to dismount, so that she was obliged with an ill grace to accept the services of her own gentleman. Nobody spoke to her, nor did she herself either speak or smile. Pepys followed the cavalcade into Whitehall, where the ladies lingered in the Queen's presence-chamber talking and laughing and trying on one another's hats. 'But it was the finest sight to me,' exclaims the susceptible diarist, 'considering their great beautys and dress, that ever I did see in all my life. But above all, Miss Stuart in this dresse, with her hat cocked and a red plume, with her sweet eye, little Roman nose, and excellent taille, is now the greatest beauty I ever saw, I think, in my life; and, if ever woman can, do exceed my Lady Castlemaine, at least in this dress: nor do I wonder if the King changes, which I verily believe is the reason of his coldness to Lady Castlemaine.'[1]

[1] Pepys July 13th, 1663.

CHAPTER III

The Court at Tunbridge—Frances in the ascendant—Her many admirers—Buckingham—His character and career—His attempt to govern the King through Frances—Mary, Duchess of Richmond—The Butterfly story—Buckingham's party for the King—Sir Henry Bennet—George Hamilton—He ingratiates himself with Frances—Interference of Gramont—The Court at Oxford—Lady Castlemaine's illness—The Court returns to London—Frances Stuart's virtue—Schemes to procure her for the King—She is advised by her mother and Henrietta Maria—The Queen's illness—Her hallucinations—Charles continues to make love to Frances—Talk of his marrying her in the event of the Queen's death—Lady Castlemaine's conversion—Charles II's. reply to her indignant relations—Recovery of the Queen—Charles still determined to make Frances his mistress.

Already in May the Queen had been anxious to go to Tunbridge Wells to take the waters, which she believed would benefit her in her present condition; but at that time the necessary funds had not been available, and it was not until the end of July that she was enabled to move her Court into the country. At this period Tunbridge was little more than a village, so that it was impossible to find lodgings there for the entire Court, and the wits and beauties of London were forced to distribute themselves among the small houses and cottages in the neighbourhood, and to endure all manner of discomforts,

But youth and gaiety can triumph over such disadvantages. The Court led a mock-arcadian existence, amusing itself in imagining a return to the Golden Age, and playing at glorified rusticity. Remembering too that the loves of shepherd and shepherdess have always been the burden of poets' songs, everyone hastened to complete the rustic illusion, and, indeed, so many reputations were lost in these halcyon days that the French ambassador declared that the waters of Tunbridge ought to be known as ' Les Eaux de Scandale.'[1]

Frances Stuart was now the goddess before whom all prostrated themselves; her every mood was reflected by the rest of the Court. It smiled with her, frowned with her, laughed with her, sighed with her. Little wonder it is that those who had great ambitions strove to gain her aid in their achievement. Foremost among these self-seeking admirers was George Villiers, Duke of Buckingham, son of the splendid favourite of James I. and Charles I. Buckingham was one of the worst and one of the most fascinating characters of his time. Destitute of principle, dissolute, and vicious, he yet possessed every attraction that would be most likely to appeal to a girl of Frances Stuart's age and temperament. To a handsome person he added many accomplishments, and his gaiety, brilliance, and extravagant

---

[1] C.A. 80. Cominges to Louis XIV, August 1663.

generosity made him one of the outstanding figures at Court. Dryden drew a superb portrait of him in the character of Zimri in the satire of 'Absolom and Achitophel.'

> ' A man so various, that he seemed to be
> Not one, but all mankind's epitome :
> Stiff in opinions, always in the wrong ;
> Was everything by starts, and nothing long ;
> But, in the course of one revolving moon,
> Was chymist, fiddler, statesman, and buffoon : '

This is severe condemnation ; but it does not appear to have been exaggerated, though Dryden might well have been excused had he been tempted to lay on the colours a little more thickly, for Buckingham, in whose armoury also ridicule was one of the chief weapons, had not spared Dryden when he drew him in the guise of the poet Bayes, for his witty comedy, ' The Rehearsal.' Horace Walpole, indeed, was of the opinion that the Duke came off best in this duel of wits. ' Zimri is an admirable portrait, but Bayes is an original creation. Dryden satirised Buckingham ; but Villiers made Dryden satirise himself.'[1]

The varied and adventurous career he had already led must have cast a romantic glamour over the Duke of Buckingham. Born in 1627, when still

---

[1] Walpole. Royal and Noble Authors.

little more than a child he had joined the Royalist forces during the Civil War, and had continued to struggle to the very end, having been one of those who had taken part in Lord Holland's belated and disastrous rising. At the defeat of Kingston his younger brother Francis was killed, but he himself escaped and for the next few months led a life of perilous adventures and hairbreadth escapes. It was characteristic both of the man's reckless bravery and of his merry impudence that he should have chosen to conceal himself in the most conspicuous place available. While the Roundhead soldiery were searching high and low for the Duke of Buckingham, his Grace was engaged in giving public performances on an open-air stage at Charing Cross. He had disguised himself as a mountebank in a Jack Pudding's coat and a ridiculous hat adorned with a fox's brush and cock's feathers, and in this egregious costume, with his face daubed either with flour or lamp-black according to his mood, he strutted about his platform, offering to do anything from telling fortunes to providing infallible remedies for any manner of disease, selling songs and ballads written by himself, and obligingly singing them to possible purchasers.[1]

After a time these proceedings became too risky to continue, or mayhap the Duke found himself unable to derive any further amusement

[1] Memoirs of the Court of England. Countess Dunois (D'Aulnoy).

from them; at any rate he determined to leave London, and succeeded in escaping to France and joining Prince Charles. His joyous personality soon made him a favourite companion of the Prince, and when, on the expedition to Scotland, the jealous and suspicious Scots removed all his friends from about him, an exception was made in favour of the Duke of Buckingham. When Charles invaded England, Buckingham was with the army and took part in the Battle of Worcester. After the defeat he again became a fugitive and went through many thrilling adventures before regaining safety in France. For some years now he followed the fortunes of the Royalist party, though his eccentricity of conduct and unstable temperament caused him to be viewed with disfavour and distrust by those about the King, and even at times by His Majesty himself. Lack of means too made life troublesome and uncongenial to one of his extravagant tastes, so to remedy this his bold spirit conceived a project even more grotesquely impertinent than any of his former exploits. Owing to his adherence to the Royalist cause his English estates had been confiscated, and a large portion of them had been granted to General Fairfax by a grateful Parliament. In Buckingham's whimsical brain there arose the fantastic notion of crossing over to England and marrying the daughter and heiress of the new owner of his ancestral estates. No sooner had he conceived the idea than he proceeded to put it into execution. Probably no other than Buckingham would have succeeded in so unusual a quest, but nothing could daunt the Duke, even the circumstances that the young lady was already promised to Lord Chesterfield, and that the banns for her marriage to him had actually been put up and already twice published. Mary Fairfax was speedily wooed and won. Fairfax himself, who could not help feeling a grudging admiration for the intrepid lover, was eventually persuaded to give his approval of the match. Cromwell, on the other hand, had come to look upon this impudent young man as dangerous, and succeeded at length in having him captured and confined in the Tower. There he remained until after the death of the Protector, when, there seeming no longer any reason for detaining him, he was released.

The Court of the Restoration welcomed him with open arms, and by the aid of his charming personality, his wit, and his irrepressible gaiety he rapidly became a leader of fashion and a boon-companion of the King. But the restless intriguing spirit of the man could ill brook a merely decorative position. Buckingham formed political ambitions. It was in furtherance of his deeply-laid schemes that he was now endeavouring to insinuate himself into the good graces of La Belle Stuart. He hoped to take advantage of the King's weakness for women and to use the new favourite as an instrument whereby to govern him. It was not difficult for a man such as him to gain the girl's favour. 'His capacity for childish amusements, his taste for amusing scandal, his gift of mimicry and his good voice made him admirably fitted for the task.'[1] He joined in her games of blindman's buff, chattered amiable nonsense with her, sang songs with her, for she was fond of music, and made her laugh with his wonderfully realistic imitations of the bigwigs of the Court. It was a constant delight to her to see him mimic the pomposity of the Chancellor Clarendon, the stateliness of the venerable Treasurer Southampton, and the portentous solemnity of Sir Henry Bennet. While he made himself every day more indispensable to the child, he was waiting eagerly for an opportunity of putting his infamous project into execution. At last he considered that the time was ripe, and drew up his plans with the aid of his wife and his sister, the Duchess of Richmond. Buckingham's wife was ready to follow wherever her lord and master led. His relations with her were somewhat similar to those subsisting between Charles and his Queen. In spite of his infidelities and neglect she adored him and had become his devoted slave, ready to pander to all his eccentricities, and, though herself naturally prone to virtue, to afford him her unstinted support in any schemes, however nefarious.

[1] Gramont. Memoirs.

The Duchess of Richmond was the eldest child of the great Duke of Buckingham, being some three or four years older than the Duke her brother. She had been married while still a child to Charles, Lord Herbert, eldest son of the Earl of Pembroke and Montgomery, and had been left a widow at the age of twelve. Charles the First then sent for her and had her brought up with the royal children at Court, where she was a conspicuous and pathetic little figure in her black garb and flowing veil. A charming tale is told of an early escapade of hers. One day she stole into the King's Privy Garden, where nobody was permitted to go, and climbed up into an apple-tree to gather some fruit. While she was still there perched among the branches, King Charles the First came into the garden, and, perceiving from a distance that some strange black creature had settled in one of the trees, he sent a favourite courtier, named Porter, to discover what it was, with instructions to shoot it and bring it to him, if it should turn out to be some rare bird, beast, or butterfly. The young man, armed with his gun, cautiously approached the tree, but great was his surprise, on drawing near, to find that the mysterious being was little Lady Herbert, who mischievously pelted him with the fruit she had gathered. The young man informed her that he had orders to shoot her and bring her to the King, but she intimated that she would prefer to be captured alive. And so it happened that a few minutes later Porter and another gentleman entered the King's apartments, each bearing one end of a large hamper. Porter informed His Majesty that the strange creature had turned out to be a butterfly, which he had captured alive, since it was so beautiful that had he killed it he would never have outlived it himself. The King was all eagerness to open the hamper and examine this rarity, but his astonishment and amusement were great when, the fastenings being undone and the lid thrown open, little Lady Herbert jumped out and threw her arms around his neck. From this time forward the heroine of this adventure was universally known as 'Butterfly.'[1] In 1637 King Charles I. married her to his kinsman James Stuart, Duke of Lennox, whom in 1641 he created Duke of Richmond. The Duke died in 1655 and left his Duchess a widow for the second time. The Duchess of Richmond was devoted to the interests of her brother, Buckingham, and possessed much of his intriguing spirit with an equal disregard for conventional morality and common decency. She was therefore not at all averse to joining in the plan which he now unfolded to her, and which was as simple as it was infamous. The two Duchesses were to give a party for the King, Frances Stuart was to be invited, and during the course of the evening an

[1] Memoirs of the Court of England. Countess Dunois. (D'Aulnoy)

opportunity was to be afforded to His Majesty of making the young girl his mistress. Whether Frances Stuart's consent was to be obtained by force or by persuasion has not been recorded, but it may be assumed that any who were likely to be scrupulous about the methods employed to overcome her reluctance, were not numbered among the guests invited to the feast. It was unfortunate for the conspirators that there was one person in England, who could dispense with the formality of an invitation and chose to exercise her prerogative on this occasion. At the very last moment the Queen, having heard that this was to be a most entertaining party, took it into her head to announce that she herself would honour it with her presence. Catherine was beginning to show a surprising firmness and independence. On this occasion she came attended only by Lady Castlemaine, refusing flatly to be followed everywhere by the vigilant eye of her Lady of the Bed-chamber, the Countess of Suffolk, and declaring that she would not always have a governess at her heels, especially in places where the King was.

Whether the Queen had any suspicion of what was afoot, or whether she acted in ignorance, merely desiring not to be left out of a party when the King was to be present, the effect was the same, for Buckingham's purpose could not be accomplished while she and Lady Castlemaine were present. The

Queen must have thought that the rumours regarding the liveliness of the party had been greatly exaggerated, as the supper proceeded in a dismal and constrained atmosphere, the discomfiture of the baffled conspirators showing itself in sullenness and silence. The King, who was always quick to see the humorous side of things, was the first to recover himself. Far from being enraged at this set back he was determined that the Queen should not be denied the reward of victory. Since she had come in search of amusement, she must not be disappointed, so, to remedy the prevailing gloom after supper, he sent for the Queen's Maids of Honour and proposed a dance. Gaiety was soon restored, and in the end all the guests enjoyed themselves so much that they did not disperse till three o'clock in the morning. The party had in the end been a great success, though scarcely in the way that had been intended by its promoters.[1]

Someone must have divulged the real object of the party, since the facts had become known to the French Ambassador, and it was possibly resentment at the trap so basely laid for her that made Frances withdraw her favour from the Duke of Buckingham, though the reason for the discontinuance of their close friendship may have been, as Gramont suggests, that the Duke had fallen seriously in love with her

---

[1] Cominges. C.A. 80. August 1663

and had made importunate advances, which had met with a severe repulse. At any rate he appeared to have abandoned, for the time being at least, all attempts to use her as a pawn in his political schemes.

But others were not to be daunted by the Duke's failure. Sir Henry Bennet, better known to fame by the title of Lord Arlington, subsequently conferred on him, was the next to make the attempt. Bennet, who had started his career as secretary to Lord Digby, Secretary of State in Charles the First's reign, had already achieved high distinction. On the outbreak of the Civil War he had abandoned civil employment in favour of the army and had fought with great gallantry, sustaining several severe wounds in the King's service. One of these, a heavy gash across the bridge of the nose, had left so hideous a scar that he always kept it covered with a narrow strip of black plaster, which gave him a somewhat peculiar appearance. During the Commonwealth he had followed the fortunes of Prince Charles, sharing his exile for a time, and then becoming the representative of his interests in Spain. When Charles was restored, the office of Keeper of the Privy Purse was bestowed on him in recognition of his services. With an ambitious man like Bennet such a post as this could only be a stepping-stone to greater things. His secret aim was to supplant Clarendon in the position of first minister, which he virtually held, and from the start he was constantly intriguing against him and endeavouring by subtle means to undermine his influence. Though not a man of brilliant genius, he had succeeded by an astute use of such qualities as he possessed in building up for himself a greater reputation than he really deserved. Such was the man who, convinced, like Buckingham, of the advisability of working upon the King's feelings by means of a female favourite, now sought an interview with Frances Stuart with the object of inducing her to afford him her good offices in this particular. 'But he was only in the preface of his speech,' says Gramont, 'when she recollected that he was at the head of those whom the Duke of Buckingham used to mimic; and as his presence and his language exactly revived the ridiculous ideas that had been given her of him, she could not forbear bursting out into a fit of laughter in his face, so much the more violent as she had for a long time struggled to suppress it.' It is small wonder that Bennet, enraged at such a reception, forthwith gave up all idea of a political alliance with so frivolous a person. Though Frances admittedly forgot her good manners on this occasion, from the very nature of his advances Bennet can hardly be considered to have merited more courteous treatment. Perhaps he himself came to that conclusion, for at all events he bore her no lasting grudge, and they became quite good friends before many months were over.

For the second time an attempt to gain an ascendancy over Frances had somehow or other miscarried. This feather-headed young creature seemed to have an extraordinary gift for thwarting all inconvenient advances, even when they were made by some of the ablest men in the country. In truth, they, like Gramont, seem to have been deceived by her apparent frivolity into thinking that she was merely foolish, and it did not occur to any of them that her childishness and careless gaiety were by no means incompatible with innate good sense in serious matters and a firmness which enabled her to resist all attempts to make her disobey the dictates of her own reason.

To the bitter disappointment of the King he was informed that the waters of Tunbridge had not had the desired effect on the Queen, and that his hope of an heir was for the moment frustrated. But the doctors were as yet full of hope, and opined that Bath might succeed where Tunbridge had failed. 'Every method of getting a successor to the English Throne is to be tried,' wrote Cominges, 'and the King on his part contributes all that could be asked of true affection and regular assiduity.'[1] As a result of the doctors' advice the Court moved westward in September.

During this autumn in the country Frances found a new admirer in young George Hamilton, second

---

[1] Cominges. August 1663. C.A. 80.

son of Sir George Hamilton, and elder brother of Elizabeth Hamilton, who afterwards became Comtesse de Gramont, and Anthony Hamilton, the writer of the Gramont memoirs. There was no element of self-interest in his love for her; he had truly fallen a victim to her beauty, her vivacity, and her artless charm. After he had frequented her apartments for days, watching for a favourable opportunity to attract her attention to him, at length his patience was rewarded. It happened one evening that old Lord Carlingford, an Irish peer, eager, like everyone else, to find diversions for the rising star, bethought himself of showing her how to hold a lighted candle in her mouth and keep the burning end there without extinguishing it. Hamilton, who boasted of an unusually capacious mouth, saw his chance, and resolved to outdo all others who should attempt the experiment. He was actually so successful as to take two candles in his mouth at the same time and walk three times round the room without putting them out. His prowess evoked universal applause; Killigrew maintained that nothing but a lantern could hope to compete with him, while Frances was so delighted that she forthwith admitted Hamilton into the innermost circle of her intimate friends. He became one of her most favoured companions, and was constantly to be found at her side in all the diversions of the Court, whether within doors or without. Hawking was the favourite field-sport of King Charles the Second, since he could never bear to be separated for long from the ladies of his Court, and it was the only form of sport which at that time was suitable for them. Frances, who adored riding, was always to be found in the brilliant cavalcade, and George Hamilton, who had taken great pains to provide her with a suitable mount, constituted himself her trusty squire, riding always by her side. On one occasion her horse took fright at the rustling of her petticoats and ran away with her. Hamilton at once dashed off in pursuit, and fortunately succeeded in catching up with her before she was thrown. Although unhurt, she was at first inclined to be dismayed, because he had been the witness of a disarray in her garments that revealed more of her figure than it was customary to display, but luckily Hamilton's tact was equal to the occasion, and his delicate handling of a somewhat embarrassing situation disposed her all the more in his favour. He now became foremost in her counsels; she trusted him with all her secrets, accepted his devotion with pleasure, and seemed to take such delight in his company that he began to think his love was returned. This thought made him lose his head altogether: in his blind infatuation he forgot the King's affection for her and was prepared to fling himself at her feet and beseech her to be his. At this point, fortunately for him, the Chevalier de Gramont, who had been anxiously watching the progress of the affair, took it upon himself to remonstrate with him on his foolhardiness, pointing out the danger of pursuing a lady, who was honoured with his Monarch's attentions. Gramont was thoroughly competent to speak on such a matter, seeing that his own presence in England was due to the fact that he had been misguided enough to make advances to Mademoiselle de la Motte Argencourt, with whom his own master, Louis XIV., was also enamoured. His logical reasoning and sensible arguments shattered Hamilton's dreams, and persuaded him to abandon his attentions. Afterwards, when he had had time for cool consideration, he was quick to acknowledge the services Gramont had rendered him. He could see now that his whole estimate of Frances Stuart's character had been false, that her familiarity with him was scarcely a sign that she entertained a passion for him, and that her acceptance of his enthusiastic admiration did not portend that any advances of a more pressing nature would be gratifying to her. It began to dawn on him that she looked upon praise and admiration as only due to her flawless beauty. It was not vanity with her so much as a sincere belief that she was perfect in beauty. Hamilton himself was convinced of her artlessness; he told Gramont ' that she was so fully acquainted with the advantages she possessed over all other women, that it was hardly possible to praise any lady at court for a well-turned arm, and a fine leg, but she was ever ready to dispute the point by demonstration, and he really believed, that, with a little address, it would not be difficult to induce her to strip naked, without ever reflecting upon what she was doing.'[1]

On the way back to London the Court halted for a few days at Oxford, a favourite city with Charles the Second, because of its unremitting loyalty to his father during the Civil War. The coming of the King and his followers was like the descent of a flock of parrots on a rookery. Aphrodite supplanted Pallas-Athene as the tutelary deity of the University, and the old grey courts of learning were now filled with a chattering throng of fair ladies and richly-clad cavaliers amongst whom His Majesty strolled with a crowd of yapping spaniels at his heels.

In all the gay multitude none was gayer or happier than Frances Stuart, for the King's admiration for her was obvious to the world, and all good courtiers were therefore lavish in their attentions to her and eager to gratify her every caprice. But though she avowedly and unaffectedly revelled in her triumph, she remained so free from vanity and arrogance that even those who most envied her could not find it in their hearts to hate her.[1] Lady Castlemaine's

---

[1] Gramont Memoirs.
[2] Cominges. September 13th, 1663. C.A. 80.

influence was no longer to be feared; her party in the Queen's household was rapidly weakening, and she herself was suffering from a quartan fever which was apparently sufficiently grave, since it was considered that it would take some three or four months to get her well again.[1]

The Court returned to London on October the 2nd. The King was every day falling more deeply in love with Frances, and she too seemed at first to encourage his advances, but only up to a point, for when he became more ardent in his wooing she drew back. After all she was only sixteen, and it is not astonishing that passion frightened her. Kisses, caresses, protestations of eternal devotion, openly-expressed admiration of her beauty, all the butterfly side of love, rejoiced her childish and romantic heart; but it is surely understandable that she should have shrunk from what, in a court so addicted to amorous intrigues and presided over by so accomplished a libertine as Charles the Second, were the almost inevitable consequences of entering into the lists of love. Her shyness only served to inflame the ardour of the King, who was accustomed to an eager acceptance of his most tentative advances. Yet at times he waxed impatient at her continued refusals to grant his desires, and he is said to have become so enraged with her obstinacy that he told her that one

---

[1] Cominges. September 13th, 1663. C.A. 80.

La Belle Stuart 61

day he hoped to see her grow old and willing. It was a perplexing situation for the King. Charles the Second may have been one of the most lecherous men who ever sat on a throne, but he was also one of the least brutal. He could never have reconciled himself to using force to obtain his will with the girl, as he easily might have done, had he wished. But he himself felt that he must attempt to procure his ends gradually by gentler means, insistent persuasions, subtle cajolements, dazzling promises. Insidious assaults of this nature must sooner or later overcome her stubborn resistance; for she had few allies, while many of His Majesty's loyal subjects were only too eager to lend their aid in this inglorious siege of a girl's virginity. Buckingham again returned to the charge. With his wife, Sir Henry Bennet, and Edward Montagu, cousin of Lord Sandwich, he formed a fresh cabal of pimps to procure Frances Stuart for the King. Their schemes were again doomed to failure; Pepys soon heard from Lord Sandwich that ' all the plot was spoiled and the whole committee broke.' This time there was no mistaking the reason why the machinations of Buckingham and his dissolute friends had miscarried. The ' beautiful fool' and ' inanimate statue ' of Gramont's estimation was proving herself an antagonist to be reckoned with. As Pepys picturesquely puts it, the truth was that Miss Stuart ' proves a cunning slut, and is advised at Somerset

House by the Queen-Mother and by her mother.'[1] In matters of this kind it would have been hard to find better counsellors than these two clever and experienced women of the world. Moreover Henrietta Maria's influence was still powerful, and she was ever willing to protect and defend Frances, for whom and for her sister, Sophia, who was one of her own 'dressers,' she possessed a great affection. Mrs. Stuart's influence was less obvious, but not less formidable; she remained a shadowy, mysterious figure always in the background, subtle and intriguing, a personality whose influence was felt rather than discerned. She had all the more reason now to counsel Frances to stiffen her resistance; for an hitherto inconceivable prospect had opened before her. The Queen was suddenly stricken with so violent a fever that her life was despaired of. The King's passion for Frances was now at its height, and it was openly asserted that, if the Queen died, he would marry her. It would be the summit of folly then, if she were by a premature surrender to jeopardize her chances of becoming Queen of England.

For days the Queen lay between life and death, while the doctors and priests wrangled over the respective merits of medical and spiritual remedies. Pigeons were slaughtered and their reeking carcases

[1] Pepys. November 6th, 1663.

La Belle Stuart 63

placed at her feet, while her head, shaved by order of the doctors, was covered by the priests with a night-cap reputed to possess miraculous powers of healing. At one time she was so weak that her death seemed certain, and extreme unction was administered to her. Her mind during her illness was constantly occupied with her desire for a child; in her delirium she imagined that she had at last given birth to an heir. Its ugliness seemed to distress her, so the King, to humour her, assured her that it was a very pretty boy. 'Nay', said the Queen, 'if it be like you, it is a fine boy indeed, and I would be very well pleased with it.'[1] During the succeeding days she imagined that she had given birth to two more children, and was delighted that the girl was so much like the King.[2]

Charles was most distressed at his Queen's illness, and his tenderness for her was increased by the knowledge of her love for him which she betrayed in her delusions. He sat constantly by her bed-side, and tearfully besought her to live for his sake. Here is another instance of the curious complexity of the King's character. Undoubtedly he was sincere in his grief and anxiety, undoubtedly he really meant what he said to the Queen, yet all the time he was pursuing Frances with his attentions. Every evening he would pass straight from the Queen's bed-side to

---

[1] Pepys. Sept. 22nd, 1663. [2] Pepys. Sept. 27th, 1663.

supper at Lady Castlemaine's, where, by his desire Frances was always present. 'The King appears to me very much afflicted,' wrote Cominges to Louis XIV, 'nevertheless he supped yesterday evening with Lady Castlemaine and conversed as usual with Mademoiselle Stuart, with whom he is very much in love. His remarriage is already discussed. Everyone chooses him a wife according to his own inclinations, and there are some who do not look for her out of England.'[1] The respect universally shown to Frances makes it quite clear that it was to her that the French Ambassador was alluding. There was little doubt in anyone's mind that the King would have married her, had the Queen died. Such a marriage would have been unusual; it would of course have caused a stir; but no doubt the importance of the distant connection of the Blantyre Stuarts with the Royal House would have been insisted upon and exaggerated, and, to allay popular scruples as to the suitability of the match, evidence of royal descent would have been ingeniously bolstered up by judicious inventions. At any rate the kinship, distant though it was, had always been admitted and stressed, and, since the first Lord Blantyre had been brought up with James I, the association of the two families had been drawn even closer.

Frances was kind to the King these days, though

[1] Cominges to Louis XIV, November 1st, 1663. C.A. 80.

CATHERINE OF BRAGANÇA
S. Verelst. National Portrait Gallery

not so kind as to imperil her chances of being raised to the throne. A calculating little minx, be it freely admitted ; but what girl would not have been as cautious in such circumstances ? Pepys was informed ' how the King is now become besotted on Mrs. Stewart, that he gets into corners, and will be with her for half an hour together, kissing her to the observation of all the world ; and she now stays by herself and expects it, as my Lady Castlemaine did use to do.'[1]

The King had not entirely deserted Lady Castlemaine. He still visited her frequently ; but the fervour of his early affection for her had been extinguished by his new love. The Lady, however, made desperate efforts to recover her ascendancy, and this autumn sprang a surprise upon the world by becoming a convert to Roman Catholicism. Her knowledge that this was the King's true religion may have contributed to her decision to take this momentous step. But if she thought that her conversion would have any effect on Charles, she was mistaken ; it merely enabled him to make a characteristic reply to her indignant relations, who had begged him to interpose his authority. He never interfered, he told them, with the souls of ladies, but only with their bodies, when they were civil enough to accept his attentions.[2]

[1] Pepys. November 7th, 1663.
[2] Cominges to Lionne, December 31st, 1663. C.A. 80.

The Queen slowly but surely recovered. The affection shown to her by her husband during the critical days of her illness had had great part in reviving her spirits and giving her new strength to fight for life. Soon she was well enough to witness, if not to join in the amusements of the Court. The King wrote to the Duchess of Orleans on the 10th of December: 'Yesterday we had a little ball in the privy chamber where she looked on, and we had many of our good faces absent, yett I assure you the assembly would not have been disliked for beauty even at Paris it selfe, for we have a great many young weemen come up since you were heere who are very handsome.'

Whatever dreams Frances may have had were shattered by the Queen's restoration to health; for she could never hope to be Queen while Catherine lived. Charles was no Henry VIII.; in his strange perverse way he was really fond of his Queen, and always rejected with contumely any suggestion of divorcing her. But if he had abandoned all idea of marrying Frances, his passion for her was undiminished, and he became all the more determined to make her his mistress.

CHAPTER IV

Charles dons a black wig and resumes his pursuit of Frances—His offers to her rejected—His divided love—Lady Castlemaine's effrontery—Rumours collected by Pepys—Anglican sermons—Frances resists the King—Miss Jennings—The story of the calash—Portraits of Frances—The Comet of 1664—Predictions of the astrologers—War with the Dutch—The célèbre ambassade extraordinaire—Courtin turns his attention to Frances—The Great Plague—The Court retires to Hampton Court—Lady Castlemaine departs to Richmond— Lely's 'Beauties'—The King and Queen at Salisbury—Frances Stuart's dream—Charles II. in Dorset—Parliament meets at Oxford—The breach with France—Strained relations between the King and his brother—Intrigues against Clarendon—The Court returns to London—General belief that Frances is the King's mistress—Clarendon's opinion—The Court in mourning—Tunbridge again—The Great Fire of London—The Persian mode introduced—Ball at Whitehall.

In proportion as the Queen regained her health and spirits, the King's revived affection for her diminished, and by the beginning of the New Year, when she was quite well again, he had already begun to relax those devoted attentions, which had contributed so much to her recovery. During the critical days of her illness his affection had been genuine enough ; for, like most cynics, Charles was thoroughly sentimental, and the spectacle of the sufferings of the woman, who, he knew, adored him had touched him so profoundly that he had found his placid half-contemptuous affection transformed for the time being into something very nearly approaching real love. There had been no insincerity in his tears over her or in his passionate prayers to her to live for his sake; his emotion had indeed been so intense as to turn his hair grey. But now that there was no longer any cause for anxiety he experienced a revulsion of feeling. The grey hair was hidden under a curling jet-black periwig of the latest fashion, and thus rejuvenated the King thrust his wife once again into the background of his life, and renewed his pursuit of Frances Stuart. So enamoured had he become that he made no attempt to conceal his feelings from the world, and sought her society quite openly. Pepys was told how the King did ' doat upon Mrs. Stewart only, and that, to the leaving of all business in the world, and to the open slighting of the Queen: that he values not who sees him, or stands by him while he dallies with her openly; then privately in her chamber below, where the very sentries observe him going in and out; and that so commonly, that the Duke, or any of the nobles, when they would ask where the King is, they will ordinarily say, ' Is the King above or below ? ' meaning with Mrs. Stewart.'[1]

Charles was dividing between three women at the

---

[1] Pepys. Jan. 20th, 1664.

same time the love that an ordinary man would devote to one at different stages of his passion. His love for Frances was romantic, it was love at its birth, an irresistible attraction towards youth and beauty and gaiety, while with the Queen it was love growing old, a tenderness free from all passion, a placid affection which was a haven for all his better instincts. But both romance and tenderness were lacking in his feelings for Lady Castlemaine; she appealed now only to that which was basest in him; the physical element, naked and undisguised, was all that survived of his former passion for her, save for a kindliness which natures like his often retain for those whom they have once loved, and which is more an effect of memory than a reflection of present feelings.

Nothing of this was hidden from Lady Castlemaine, whom long experience had endowed with an acute insight into the state of the King's feelings. She knew that she no longer possessed any influence over him, and she knew why. But if she herself was aware that she was no longer a power with the King, she was determined that others should not realize her position. To show the world that she was not yet out of favour she one day boldly entered the royal box at the theatre, and seated herself between the King and the Duke of York, who were so embarrassed and surprised that they could offer no protest.[1]

[1] Pepys. February 1st, 1664.

The industrious Pepys duly scavenged every scandalous titbit that he could hear from the Court gossips concerning the King's relations with Frances. There were plenty of ill-natured rumours afloat in these days. It was, for instance, asserted that the King had dissipated the Queen's dowry in lavish grants to Frances and Lord Fitzharding and other favourites.[1] Stories such as these could not but be apocryphal, and were merely invented as plausible explanations of the disappearance of the money. The truth of the matter was that there had been very little money to disappear, because the Queen-Regent of Portugal had only paid a small proportion of the dowry, and had ever after been unwilling or unable to redeem her promise to pay the rest. Frances in any case would never consent to receive grants from the King, if only because she knew full well the sort of conditions that would be attached to her acceptance. She steadfastly refused all gifts from Charles, save those which the custom of the age allowed young ladies to receive without any implication on particular occasions such as occurred about now, when Charles was her valentine. On this time-honoured day most of the ladies at Court received magnificent and costly gifts from their chosen Cavaliers. There is likely to be more truth in the rumour that the Queen would often hesitate

---

[1] Pepys. February 8th, 1664.

before going into her own dressing-room, for fear of finding her husband there dallying with Frances. Catherine's innate common sense had shown her that, if she wished to preserve her own dignity, it would be most politic for her to avoid seeing things which she could not prevent. At any rate Frances was less to be feared than Lady Castlemaine; she was only a thoughtless girl, and had so far shown no disposition to give her real cause for jealousy.

The gossip told to Pepys was enough to arouse in him a great interest in Frances Stuart. He sought every opportunity of seeing her; but, though he found her beautiful, she could not yet dislodge Lady Castlemaine from the first place in his estimation. 'Methinks,' he sighed regretfully, 'Mrs. Stuart is grown fatter, and not so fair as she was.' Nevertheless she was still fair enough to draw from him expressions of admiration, when he saw her at the theatre, amongst the Queen's ladies walking in the Park, or in the Queen's apartments in the Palace, where the Court gathered after morning service on Sundays.[1] Frances, being a Roman Catholic, attended the Queen's private chapel, and so escaped the lengthy and tedious sermons with which the Anglican divines of this period were wont to inflict the Court. Charles II. himself stifled his boredom in a very human manner. 'We have the same

[1] Pepys. April 1st, May 2nd, June 29th, 1664.

disease of sermons that you complaine of there,' he once wrote to his sister, ' but I hope you have the same convenience that the rest of the family has of sleeping out most of the time, which is a great ease to those who are bounde to hear them.'[1] Evelyn's description of the sermon with which the King had been regaled on the previous Sunday is certainly calculated to arouse sympathy with His Majesty's point of view. ' Dr. Fell, Canon of Christ Church, preached before the King, on the 15 ch Romans, v. 2, a very formal discourse, and in blank verse, according to his manner; however, he is a good man.'[2]

In her treatment of the King Frances Stuart was undoubtedly playing a very dangerous game. She was fully determined never to surrender to him, and yet she felt that she could not afford to let him abandon his pursuit, and must therefore never allow him to despair utterly of winning her. The King's continued relations with Lady Castlemaine did not alarm her, for she knew that all romance had long ago departed from them; danger could come only from a rival who could arouse the King's tenderness as well as inflame his passions. It was with the appearance at Court of Frances Jennings, a lively young lady, whose gaiety and charm rivalled her own, that she found her own supremacy for the

[1] Charles II. to Madame. February, 28th, 1666.
[2] Evelyn. February 24th, 1666.

first time seriously threatened. She was not too cold to be jealous, and, though unwilling to become the King's mistress herself, was not prepared to surrender him to someone who would be more accommodating. The Duke of York had at once fallen a victim to the charms of Miss Jennings, who had been appointed a Maid of Honour to his wife, and Frances saw with alarm that the King too was beginning to show signs of a dawning interest in her. She at once determined that the affair must be allowed to go no further, and tartly suggested that His Majesty should confine his attentions to the ladies of his own household, and leave the Duchess's Maids of Honour free for the Duke. In case this somewhat Oriental suggestion should prove ineffective, she reinforced it with threats to marry and retire from Court. She was running a great risk by making such suggestions, but apparently she knew her man. The King's interest in Miss Jennings died away as quickly as it had arisen.

Another story shows, if it be true, how unscrupulous Frances had become in her efforts to get her own way with Charles. The Chevalier de Gramont presented the King with a magnificent calash with glass windows, the first of its kind ever seen in England. 'The Queen, imagining that so splendid a carriage might prove fortunate for her, wished to appear in it first, with the Duchess of York. Lady Castlemaine, who had seen them in it, thinking that it set off a fine figure to greater advantage than any other, desired the King to lend her this wonderful calash to appear in it the first fine day in Hyde Park. Miss Stewart had the same wish; and requested to have it on the same day. As it was impossible to reconcile these two goddesses, whose former union was turned into mortal hatred, the King was very much perplexed.

Lady Castlemaine was with child, and threatened to miscarry, if her rival was preferred. Miss Stewart threatened that she never would be with child, if her request was not granted: this menace prevailed, and Lady Castlemaine's rage was so great, that she had almost kept her word; and it was believed that this triumph cost her rival some of her innocence.'[1]

How much truth there is in this tale, it is difficult to say, but certain it is that Charles never got his reward—if it was ever promised. Unfortunately it cannot be disguised that Frances was perfectly capable of making such promises without any intention of fulfilling them. She was well aware that Charles was too gentle and easy-going to force any woman against her inclinations, and that it would be easy to make him feel that it would be brutal to persist. She could not conceal from herself that one day the King's patience would reach its limits, but she was confident of being able to keep

[1] Gramont. Memoirs.

La Belle Stuart

him at arm's length for the present, and into the future she did not care to look. So long as she was able she would devote herself to enjoying life, and she threw herself heart and soul into an endless succession of gaieties. The wonderful weather in this summer of 1664 threw a glamour of poetry over these days. The Court took most of its diversions on the water, rowing down to Greenwich or up to Hampton Court, and supping gaily in the cool of the evening on the homeward journey beneath the stars. To be the admired of all on such romantic occasions was the very zenith of happiness to a girl of Frances Stuart's butterfly nature. She asked for nothing more ; she wanted the roses of love without its realities.

The desire of painters to set Frances Stuart's beauty on record for posterity must have given peculiar pleasure to her. She was frequently painted about this time. On July 15th Pepys, waiting for a friend in one of the galleries of White Hall saw coming ' out of the chayre-room Mrs. Stewart, in a most lovely form, with her hair all about her eares, having her picture taking there. There was the King and twenty more, I think, standing by all the while, and a lovely creature she in the dress seems to be.' Some weeks later[1] Pepys saw another portrait of her. 'To see some pictures at one Huysman's a picture-

---

[1] Pepys. August 26th, 1664.

drawer, a Dutchman, which is said to exceed Lilly: and indeed there is both of the Queens and Maids of Honour, particularly Mrs. Stewart's in a buff doublet like a soldier, as good pictures, I think as ever I saw.' This curious and fascinating portrait is now in the Royal Collection at Buckingham Palace. Frances is habited as a man, with golden periwig and gold-hilted sword. Her buff doublet is adorned with bows of blue ribbon, and the outer sleeves are decorated with strips of dull golden braid. Masquerading in male attire seems not to have been uncommon among ladies at Court in this reign. An account of W. Watts, mercer to the Duchess of Portsmouth, contains elaborate articles of male attire, as ' a coat of pigeon-breast and silver brocade, . . . breeches having at the thigh slashed seams to show red and silver lace.'[1] The fashion has been attributed to Nell Gwynne's success on the stage dressed as a man in Florimel and other characters, but it seems to have come in earlier, since this portrait was painted a year or so previously to the appearance on the stage of ' pretty, witty Nelly.'

The superstition of the time discerned in the comet, which appeared in the autumn of 1664, a herald of misfortune. Astrologers foretold war, fire, pestilence, and famine; some even went so far as to proclaim that the world was coming to an end in

---

[1] Forneron. Louise de Keroualle.

"MRS. STEWART, IN A BUFF DOUBLET LIKE A SOLDIER"
Jacob Huysman, Buckingham Palace

1666—a prediction which contributed exceedingly to the alarm of the ignorant, especially when their other terrible prophecies were one by one fulfilled during the course of the next two years. To foretell war in the immediate future scarcely needed a gift of prophecy; for commercial and colonial jealousy between the English and Dutch had already led to hostilities in America and the Indies on several occasions, and nearer home the ever-vexed question of the ' Dominion of the Seas ' was always present. It was merely a question of time before there would be an open rupture. Although Louis XIV. had dreaded nothing more than an alliance between the two maritime powers, he pretended that he was most reluctant to see war between them. But, as a matter of fact, it was not inconvenient to him that England and Holland should weaken one another, so long as they did not allow their war to interfere with his cherished designs on the Spanish Netherlands. Concluding therefore that, in case an opportunity should arise of putting them into execution, he must place himself in the position of being able to stop the war at any moment, he expressed himself much dismayed when England declared war against Holland in March 1665, and hastened to offer his mediation. Two additional ambassadors were sent over to England to join with Cominges in attempting to persuade Charles II. to open negotiations with the Dutch. A certain complexity was added to the situation in that the envoys, not being admitted into Louis's secrets, were obviously sincere in their efforts for peace.

The two new members of the embassy, which is known to history as the 'célèbre ambassade extraordinaire,' were Henri de Bourbon, Duc de Verneuil, and Honoré de Courtin. In sending Verneuil Louis XIV. doubtless wished to give the impression that he attached great importance to the embassy. The Duke was a son of Henry IV. by Henriette de Balzac d'Entragues, and was therefore half-brother to Henrietta Maria and uncle to the Kings of England and France. Born in 1601 he had first adopted an ecclesiastical career, becoming successively Abbé de St. Germain and Bishop of Metz, but later he had decided to return to the world, and had been created Duc de Verneuil by Louis XIV. He was an extremely handsome man, and likely to commend himself to the English, since he was a keen sportsman. Although he was by no means merely a figurehead, the actual work of the negotiation was to fall chiefly upon Cominges and Courtin, 'conseiller en tous les conseils,' and a very able diplomatist. The embassy arrived in April.

Courtin was fully cognizant of the importance of feminine influence at the Court of England, and without delay proceeded to study the characters of the reigning beauties, and examine the possibilities of deriving any assistance from them. He had seen

Frances Stuart as a child, and was astonished to find how she had changed. 'Yesterday,' he wrote, ' I saw one of his mistresses, whom I should not have recognized, she has grown so much taller and more beautiful since she left the Palais-Royal : it is of Mademoiselle Stuart I would speak, who is assuredly the prettiest girl at this Court and would pass for a very great beauty in any country.' Lady Castlemaine he had not yet seen, but Lord Falmouth had promised to introduce him at the earliest opportunity. He was convinced that both the ladies were the King's mistresses, and suspected him of other affairs as well.[1]

While the Court at Whitehall was thus occupying itself with love and politics, a terrible enemy was insidiously creeping into the town about it. This was the Plague, which was supposed to have been introduced from Holland, where there had recently been a serious epidemic. Possibly because the contagion is carried by a seafaring folk, the rats, maritime nations seem always to have been peculiarly subject to such outbreaks. At first the cases were few and far between, but they gradually increased in number until the outbreak assumed alarming proportions. Every effort was made to stem the tide of the disease by shutting up infected houses, but all precautions were unavailing, and soon the

[1] Courtin to Lionne. April, 1662. C.A. 80.

list of the dead ran into thousands every week. Trade was at a standstill, and all who could possibly do so fled from London. The Court took the natural but scarcely popular course of withdrawing itself from infection on the earliest opportunity, and removed in June to Hampton Court, with the intention of moving further afield if it should be necessary.

To find accommodation for everyone at Hampton Court itself was out of the question, so that many people had to be content with lodgings in neighbouring places. The French Ambassadors, to their great disgust, were quartered at Kingston, several miles away. Courtin was seriously applying himself to the task of counteracting Spanish influence at Court. Since the Spanish ambassador, the Count de Molina, had succeeded in ingratiating himself with Lady Castlemaine, Courtin resolved to win the good graces of La Belle Stuart, and attach her, if possible, to the French interest. Her upbringing in France had bred in her a great affection for the French, whose language she spoke as well as or even better than her own, so that it was no difficult task for Courtin to capture her sympathy. Finding that flattery was always acceptable to her, Courtin, who possessed to the full the gift of his race for framing graceful compliments, speedily won his way into her favour by his openly-expressed admiration of her beauty. Not that Frances could in any sense have been called an agent of the French party; Courtin knew better than to try to derive any actual assistance from her; since she avowedly abhorred politics, and could never be persuaded to enter into any political intrigues. All that he required of her was that she should like him personally enough to seek his society, and so provide him with frequent opportunities of meeting the King informally in her apartments. Time was pressing, as it was obvious to the French envoys that the more successful England was in the war, the less likely Charles was to accept French mediation. The Duke of York had won a signal naval victory early in June, and, though the Dutch did not seem greatly discouraged thereby, further English successes would render useless the continuance of the negotiations. The French sorely needed every friend they could obtain; for the general attitude of the English towards them was one of profound mistrust. With unusual acumen the populace suspected that, though the French outwardly professed friendship for England, they were secretly encouraging the Dutch. Courtin wrote to Lionne, informing him of the alarming headway which the Spanish party was making by means of bribery. 'As for us whom the English do not salute in the streets and who have no one now whom we can trust, we are obliged to give incense[1] instead of money. This offering has sufficed so far with Miss Stuart, to whose apartments

---

[1] i.e. flattery.

the King of England took me yesterday evening at 11 o'clock, and I can assure you that I am on better terms with her than the Count de Molina is with Lady Castlemaine. She is the rising sun, and in truth too is incomparably more beautiful than the other. If I had not noticed in the accounts I made up yesterday that the Embassy up to now has cost me 12000 crowns of my own money over and above what it has pleased the King to give me, I should have had some embroidered waistcoats sent for her for the hunting we are going to get at Salisbury. But it does not become the younger son of a poor family to undertake this sort of gallantry, especially when he has the prospect of finding himself with four children on his hands.[1]

The machinations of the French ambassador received considerable help from an unexpected quarter by the conduct of Lady Castlemaine, who, declaring that her apartments at Hampton Court were not ready to sleep in, betook herself off to Richmond. Nobody was deceived by her excuse; a retreat to Richmond was notoriously a sign of one of the Lady's periodical fits of sulkiness. But gone were the days when Charles used to dash off in hot pursuit and fling himself at her feet beseeching her to return. Now he did not seem to resent her absence; he found pleasure and amusement enough

[1] Courtin to Lionne. July 9th, 1665. C.A. 86.

in gay supper-parties with Frances Stuart and Lord Arlington. Courtin was delighted at Lady Castlemaine's self-imposed exile; the removal of so important an ally of the Spanish party gave the French more frequent opportunities of pressing their suit with the King. Lady Castlemaine could gain nothing now by the means which formerly had served her so well; she only succeeded in irritating the King, and there was danger that her persistent ill humours would sooner or later exasperate him to such a point that he would dismiss her altogether. Such at least was Courtin's opinion. ' If her temper continues,' he wrote to Lionne, ' she may perhaps lose the best rose out of her hat. This comparison is not inapt in a country where all women wear them.'[1]

It was probably during this summer at Hampton Court that the famous series of ' Beauties ' was painted by Lely at the command of the Duchess of York. All the affectation of the time is enshrined in this collection of the loveliest women at Court masquerading as heathen goddesses or Christian saints. Here are Anne Hyde herself, Lady Castlemaine as proud Minerva, the exquisite Brooke sisters, Lady Whitmore and Lady Denham, the Countess of Falmouth, the noble Countess of Sunderland, pretty Miss Hamilton in rose-coloured draperies, and, perhaps most charming of all, Frances

---

[1] Courtin to Lionne. July 16th, 1665. C.A. 86.

Stuart, in palest yellow satin, bearing in her hand a bow, the emblem of Diana. Was it mere hazard that prompted Frances to choose to be represented as the chaste huntress?

By the end of July the Plague was raging furiously in London, and Hampton Court could no longer be considered safe. It was resolved therefore to move further afield. The Duke and Duchess of York seized the opportunity to make a tour in the North, while the King and Queen with the rest of the Court proceeded westward. At Farnham Castle Charles parted with the Queen in order to pay a visit of inspection to the fortifications in Portsmouth and the Isle of Wight. Catherine went on to Salisbury, where on her arrival she was presented by the Mayor with a handsome pair of silver flagons to show the town's due appreciation of the honour that was being conferred upon it by its being made the seat of the Court.[1] The King arrived a few days later. The most stringent precautions against the Plague were taken at Salisbury. The King caused a list of all persons necessarily and immediately relating to the Court to be delivered to the Mayor, and all strangers were forbidden the town.[2] The horror of the Plague had fastened on all men, and the number of those who were disinterested enough to remain in plague-

---

[1] The Newes. August 3rd, 1665.
[2] The Intelligence. August 7th, 1665.

stricken areas, if they could possibly avoid it, were remarkably few.

Though many lesser officials such as Evelyn and Pepys stuck to their posts throughout the scourge, few really prominent personages were ready to face the appalling danger, save the Duke of Albemarle, who remained in London as the King's representative, and the Archbishop of Canterbury, who, in spite of all remonstrances, persisted in residing at Lambeth Palace as an example to the London Clergy. Lord Craven too was a notable and a noble exception, since of his own accord he stayed in the plague-stricken city, with rare devotion risking his life and spending his substance in unselfish efforts to alleviate the suffering and distress.

But although the Court could deem itself more or less secure at Salisbury from the peril of the Plague, it can hardly be said that the visit there was an unqualified success. 'The sojourn in this place does not please their Britannic Majesties,' wrote Bigorre, secretary to the French Ambassadors, in a report to Lionne, ' it is situated very low : streams of water run along the middle of the streets : the winds are continual, and reign here with tyranny.'[1] His spirits damped by the humidity of the atmosphere, the King at one time contemplated removing to Wilton, the seat of Lord Pembroke, not far distant

[1] August 15th, 1665. C.A. 86.

But this intention was effectively foiled by Lady Castlemaine, who flatly refused to go, and this time gained her point. Charles would probably not have been so readily influenced by Lady Castlemaine's petulance, had Frances Stuart been willing to grant him the last favours, and so destroy his sole need for the Lady's presence. But she still resisted all his advances, although he had even more opportunities than usual of pressing his suit, since, while the rest of the Maids of Honour were distributed among private houses in the town, she alone was quartered in the royal lodgings.[1]

Courtin relates a characteristic anecdote of her at this time : ' The day before yesterday Miss Stuart dreamed that she was in bed with the three French Ambassadors : it is true that as she was telling the King of England about it, he called me to them, and so she blushed and said that she was next to M. de Verneuil.'[2] The Duke, of course, was the oldest of the three ambassadors ! Courtin was much amused at this dream, which he regarded as an appropriate symbol of the political relationship he was trying to bring about between Frances Stuart and the French Embassy. He continued to court her favour with assiduity, giving supper-parties for her, and asserting that one could not dine in better company even in Paris.[3]

[1] Courtin to Lionne. August 23rd, 1665. C.A. 86.
[2] Courtin to Lionne. August 23rd, 1665. C.A.
[3] Courtin to Lionne. September 13th. C.A. 86.

The King was feeling far from well, and was growing restless and depressed at Salisbury. On September the 9th he wrote to Madame saying that he proposed ' to make a little turne into dorset sheere for 8 or 9 dayes to passe away the time till I go to Oxford, believeing that this place was the cause of my indisposition.' Some days elapsed before he could finally make up his mind to take his departure, which the French Ambassadors announce in a despatch of September the 20th. ' Meanwhile the King of England, who thinks that the air of this town is not good for his health, leaves to-morrow to go and stay four or five days at my Lord Ashley's, and from there to journey for about the same length of time along the coast. Probably he will grow tired of going ten or twelve days without seeing the ladies, for they remain with the Queen, who goes hunting almost every day after dinner, or to play bowls, which is one of the chief amusements in this country.'[1] Two days later Courtin reaffirmed his opinion that the King's absence would be short : ' If one can believe a pretty girl who ought to know the truth, the King of England's journey will only last for seven or eight days.'[2] It is not difficult to guess the identity of Courtin's ' pretty girl.'

The King spent a few days with Lord Ashley at

[1] C.A. 86.   [2] C.A. 86.

St. Giles', and afterwards made a progress through some of the Dorsetshire towns. The change evidently did him good, for he returned to Salisbury ' in better disposition (God be praised), then when he went from hence.'[1]

In view of the persistence of the Plague it was decided that the Parliament should meet at Oxford this autumn. From the French Ambassadors' point of view the success or failure of their negotiation depended entirely on the humour of that Parliament, as it had become obvious that the King of England would not listen to the representations of France, if his own subjects would give him money with which to prosecute the Dutch War. Louis XIV. was now beginning to unmask his real intentions. He informed Charles that, if he would not accept his meditation, France would be obliged to support the Dutch. Charles II. told his Parliament candidly that the continuance of the Dutch war meant war with France also, and threw himself on their mercy. They responded generously with a grant of £1,250,000. After this it was useless for the French Ambassadors to remain any longer, and they took leave of the English Court, though in friendly fashion ; for they had won universal respect by their personal sincerity.

The Duke and Duchess of York had joined the

[1] The Intelligence. September 25th (os) 1665.

La Belle Stuart   89

King at Oxford, and, if Pepys, or rather his informant, Lord Sandwich, is to be credited, relations between the royal brothers were somewhat strained this autumn. 'As an infinite secret, my Lord tells me the factions are high between the King and the Duke, and all the Court are in an uproar with their loose amours; the Duke of York being in love desperately with Mrs. Stewart, Nay, that the Duchess herself is fallen in love with her new Master of the Horse, one Harry Sidney, and another Harry Savill. So that God knows what will be the end of it. . . The Duke's amours to Mrs. Stewart are told the King; so that all is like to be nought among them.'[1]

It is quite possible that the Duke had fallen in love with Frances, but it is difficult to believe that his advances to her would have greatly alarmed the King, who knew well that so vivacious a young lady was not likely to be attracted by anyone of so solemn and serious a character as His Grace of York. The brief coolness between the King and his brother was due to a very different cause—His Majesty's refusal to make Sir George Saville a viscount at the Duke's request. It was true enough that the factions were high at Court; for Clarendon's enemies had been active of late, and had almost succeeded in engineering a quarrel between him and the Treasurer.

[1] Pepys. November 17th, 1665.

Lady Castlemaine and Sir William Coventry, aided by Arlington, who, however, kept himself in the background as much as possible, were taking every opportunity to undermine Clarendon's influence. They had observed that Charles was beginning to chafe under the restrictions imposed on him by this old and faithful servant, and were prepared to stop at nothing in their endeavours to secure his dismissal.

By the beginning of the New Year (1666) the plague was almost entirely stamped out, and gradually people began to return to London. The King himself arrived at Hampton Court on January the 29th. ' I have left my wife at Oxford,' he wrote to Madame, ' but hope (that) in a fortnight or three weekes to send for her to London where already the Plague is in effect nothing, but our women are afraide of the name of plague so that they must have a little time to fancy all cleere.' On February the 2nd he proceeded to Whitehall, where he was joined by the Queen and her ladies nearly three weeks later.

It was now commonly believed that Frances Stuart was the King's mistress, although people who were unwise enough to proclaim the fact would quite conceivably find themselves in jail for libel, which was the fate of one John Davis, who ' had upbraided the King about Lady Castlemaine and Mrs. Steward and showed scandalous letters about the particulars.'[1] Pepys wrote in his diary ' how for

[1] Cal. Stat. Pap. Dom, 187, 169.

La Belle Stuart

certain Mrs. Stewart is become the King's mistress.'[1] But then Pepys's diary was not intended to be read by anyone else.

Clarendon, who should have had opportunities of knowing the truth, was unwilling to commit himself either way on the subject of Frances Stuart's virtue. But he took as little interest as he could in the amorous intrigues at Court, and never troubled to ascertain the exact nature of her relations with the King. He was certainly wrong in his estimate of Lady Castlemaine's position at this period, for, though she was still the King's mistress, her influence over him was nothing like what it had been. ' The Lady,' he says, ' who had never declined in favour, was now greater in power than ever : she was with child again, and well enough contented that his majesty should entertain an amour with another lady, and made a very strict friendship with her,[2] it may be the more diligently out of confidence that he would never prevail with her, which many others believed too. But without doubt the King's passion was stronger towards that other lady, than ever it was to any other woman : and she carried it with that discretion and modesty, that she made no other use of it than for the convenience of her own fortune

---

[1] Pepys, April, 15th, 1666.

[2] This passage exactly explains the relationship between Frances Stuart and Lady Castlemaine in 1662, four years previously. It was far otherwise now.

and subsistence, which was narrow enough ; never seemed disposed to interpose in the least degree in business, nor to speak ill of any body ; which kind of nature and temper the more inflamed the King's affection, who did not in his nature love a busy woman, and had an aversion from speaking with any woman, or hearing them speak, of any business but to that purpose he thought them all made for, however they broke in afterwards upon him to all other purposes.'[1]

In days when love-affairs of this kind were rarely if ever concealed, it seems astonishing that any doubt should have existed as to whether Frances Stuart was the King's mistress. Most people unquestioningly assumed—and, in most cases, with justice—that the King never made advances to any lady in vain. Why then should there have been a doubt in this single instance ? Truly it would appear that those who believed that the King had not prevailed with her were justified in their opinion of her virtue—unless, of course, she had actually succeeded in persuading him to keep his success with her a secret. But what could she expect to gain by this ? Such hypocrisy would not restore her self-respect, if she had fallen, and no one else cared a straw whether she were chaste or not. It would have been merely ridiculous to make a fetish of what in

[1] Clarendon, Continuation 858,

Charles II's Court was accounted the most disagreeable and contemptible of virtues in a pretty woman.

It is far more likely that Frances was truly as chaste as she pretended to be. Yet her virtue is not easy to account for; since outwardly she did not give the impression that she possessed a cold nature. When she had first come to Court she was little more than a child, and it was only to be expected that she should have shrunk from the deeper mysteries of passion, but now that she had reached an age when it is natural to love, some further explanation must be found for her reluctance. Judging from her frivolous behaviour, the King might well have been excused for being sanguine of her eventual compliance with his desires. She had never seemed unapproachable; on the contrary she had not only accepted his advances, but had even deliberately encouraged them. Nor had she seemed at all averse to attracting other admirers. Her coyness would not have seriously perturbed an experienced lover like the King, who had always had good reason for believing that:

Maids' nays are nothing; they are shy
But to desire what they deny.

It is scarcely to be wondered at then that he was amazed when he found that Frances Stuart's reluctance was not feigned, and that passion was truly distasteful to her. Virtuous she certainly was;

but it is strange that virtue should have been so easy for one of her apparent nature. Yet she never seems to have been tempted. There may be some physiological explanation of her coldness, something lacking in her which caused her to look upon passion with fear and disgust. It is possible that this incompleteness of nature on the sexual side is to be attributed to some constitutional delicacy; since her health was never robust; her radiant gaiety and spirited vivacity seem to have been the result of a highly-strung and nervous temperament rather than the natural outcome of the rude good health of youth.

The death of Queen Catherine's mother, the Queen Regent of Portugal, plunged the English Court into mourning this spring. Black evidently suited Frances Stuart, since for once Pepys was forced to admit that he found her fairer than Lady Castlemaine. ' Thence with my Lord Brouncker in his coach to Hide Parke, the first time I have been there this year. There the King was; but I was sorry to see my Lady Castlemaine; for the mourning forcing all the ladies to go in black, with their hair plain and without spots, I find her to be a much more ordinary woman than ever I durst have thought she was; and, indeed, is not so pretty as Mrs. Stuart.'[1] Such occasions as these gave their opportunity to those

[1] Pepys. April 21st, 1666.

who had been fortunate enough to have been brought up in France, and had so acquired that air of dress which can only be learnt there ! Frances was able to show the ladies of England that she was not so dependent as they were on colour and elaborate ornament, and that the admirable way in which she dressed was due less to her actual clothes than to her manner of putting them on.

The Court paid another visit to Tunbridge this summer. The days passed gaily enough with entertainments of every sort. The players were even sent for from London in order that the Court should not lack one of its favourite diversions during its enforced absence from the Capital. Gramont, indeed, suggests that the Queen's motive for sending for the players may have been ' to retort upon Miss Stuart, by the presence of Nell Gwynne, part of the uneasiness she felt from hers.' But this is a mistake,[1] for it was fully a year later that Nell Gwynne first appeared to captivate the King's affections. The simpler explanation is the more probable, because the Queen had by now herself entirely succumbed to the passion for amusement, which was one of the chief characteristics of her husband's court.

[1] The chronology of the Memoirs does not pretend to be exact. Hamilton admits that they were written to amuse rather than to instruct. Inaccuracies abound. For instance, Lord and Lady Muskerry figure in an incident during this visit to Tunbridge (1666), although Lord Muskerry had been killed in the sea-fight against the Dutch in the preceding year.

Frances was now at last forced to realize that the hour was drawing near when she would no longer be able to put the King off. Scruples may have restrained his ardour while she was still a child, but now the lovely child had grown into a beautiful young woman. The transformation was not altogether pleasing to Pepys, for he notes with regret that though she was 'a woman of most excellent features,' she had 'grown a little too tall.'[1]

In the autumn of this year there came to pass the last of the evils foretold by the astrologers as a consequence of the appearance of the comet of 1664. At two o'clock on a Sunday morning a fire began in a baker's shop in Pudding Lane in the City of London, and with the help of a high wind speedily spread to the surrounding buildings, which were chiefly of timber. All attempts to quench the flames with the primitive appliances then in use were fruitless; soon the fire spread over a vast area, making the night as light as day for a radius of ten miles. For five days and nights it raged uninterruptedly, devouring every building that it came across, private houses, shops, warehouses, churches, even the old Cathedral of St. Paul. It was feared at one time that the conflagration would spread to Whitehall, and some of the more valuable of the royal treasures were sent to Hampton Court for safety. The King raised himself

[1] Pepys. August 17th, 1666.

La Belle Stuart

in the estimation of his subjects by his courage and promptitude at this crisis. Regardless of the danger from burning and falling houses, he rode about the City on a white horse, directing operations and encouraging those who were trying to combat the terrible enemy by blowing up with gunpowder buildings that the flames had not yet reached, and thus creating a belt of waste land over which the fire could not proceed, since there was nothing left to burn. The good impression His Majesty had created was further enhanced by his solicitude for the thousands of homeless people.

Pepys had amused himself at intervals during the past year or so in comparing the respective charms of Frances Stuart and Lady Castlemaine, but on October 3rd he was reluctantly obliged to confess that neither found favour in his sight. 'To White Hall, and there, among the ladies, and saw my Lady Castlemaine never looked so ill, nor Mrs. Stuart neither, as in this plain natural dress, I was not pleased with either of them.'[1]

Costume was a matter of supreme importance at the Court of Charles the Second. Owing to the fact that England was at war with France the King felt that French fashions should no longer be followed at his Court, and in full Council declared his intention of setting a new fashion in clothes, which he would

[1] Pepys. October 3rd, 1666.

never alter. This resolution caused so much amusement at Court that many wagers were made as to the length of time during which His Majesty would succeed in keeping to it. Evelyn describes the new fashion as being after the Persian mode. ' It was a comely and manly habit,' he says, ' too good to hold, it being impossible for us in good earnest to leave the Monsieur's vanities long.'[1] The fashion was not of long duration, being speedily killed by ridicule both from this side of the Channel and the other. As the Court was in mourning the dress had necessarily to be black, relieved, if at all, by white, whereupon Charles declared that his Court looked as if it was tenanted by magpies. The King of France added the last touch by causing all his footmen to be put into the new English fashion. From the moment that the tidings of ' this ingenious kind of affront ' reached England the new fashion was doomed.[2]

In spite of the war with the French and Dutch, and in spite of such disasters as the Plague and the Great Fire, not for a moment did the Court cease its quest of pleasure. Never had it been so gay as it was this autumn. Balls, masquerades, plays, or gaming parties were held every night. A particularly magnificent ball was given at Whitehall on the Queen's birthday, November 15th. The regulations as to mourning were relaxed for the occasion, and

---

[1] Evelyn. October 30th, 1666.
[2] Pepys. Oct., 1666 (*Passim*). Evelyn, Oct., 1666 (*Passim*).

once again brilliant colours were brought out. The King, the Duke of York, and the rest of the gentlemen shone in cloth of silver, rich silks, and gold lace, while the ladies were bedizened with jewels, which sparkled in the brilliant light of thousands of candles. The Queen alone, out of respect for her dead mother, was simply attired and wore no jewels. La Belle Stuart, on the other hand, outshone everyone else in black and white lace, with diamonds glimmering on her shoulders and in her hair. She was one of the best dancers at Court, and was able, as at Monmouth's wedding, to display her grace in the Brantles, Corantos, French dances, and country dances before the jealous eyes of Lady Castlemaine, who was again expecting a child, and was therefore constrained to be an onlooker.

The King's renewed energy in the pursuit of Frances was remarked by everyone. It was generally thought that he was conducting an intrigue with her, since he devoted all his attention to her and neglected Lady Castlemaine.[1] He was more anxious than ever to possess her now that she was at the zenith of her beauty, 'I saw Mrs. Stuart this afternoon,' exclaims Pepys, 'methought the beautifullest creature that ever I saw in my life, more than ever I thought her, so often as I have seen her ; and I do begin to think do exceed my Lady Castlemaine at least now.'[2]

[1] Pepys. October 15th, December 12th, 1666.
[2] Pepys. November 25th, 1666.

CHAPTER V

The King's persistence—Frances contemplates marriage—The Duke of Richmond—His character—He proposes to marry Frances—Lady Castlemaine betrays them to the King—Frances appeals to the Queen—Charles affects to countenance the match—The elopement—The King's anger—Frances Stuart's own version of the facts—The Richmond marriage occasions the fall of Clarendon—His unpopularity and the intrigues against him—The King suspects Lord Cornbury of complicity in the elopement—Clarendon's letter to the King—Fall of Clarendon.

The King's unrequited desire for Frances was wearing him out; his patience was strained almost to breaking-point, and he became restless, distracted, and melancholy. He had tried every possible means of winning her love, and he had failed. He had laid his heart at her feet, and she had spurned it. Neither could wealth buy what his personality could not earn. He would have wished her to respond to his love, but he was willing to take her without love on her part. He offered to make her a duchess; he offered her lands and great wealth; he swore that, if she would be his, he would dismiss Lady Castlemaine and all his other mistresses.[1] In the face even of these glittering prospects Frances remained inflexible. But the strain was beginning to tell on her

[1] Burnet. History of His Own Time. Memoirs of Gramont.

also, and his very persistence became as trying to her as it was to him. In spite of her resolution she felt that her powers of resistance were gradually weakening. It is, indeed, amazing that so frail a girl should have had the strength to hold out for as long as she did ; but now she had to admit that the climax had been reached. Either she must give in, or the King would be driven to such a point of desperation that he would throw to the wind the honourable scruples that had hitherto restrained him, and force her to his will. She recognized quite frankly that she had only herself to blame for the situation in which she found herself. Though she had all along firmly resolved never to become the King's mistress, she had always encouraged him to believe that one day she would yield to his entreaties. By this somewhat callous device she had for years enjoyed all the advantages that she would have had, if she had become the King's mistress. It is true that she had given him more than she had ever given any man, but Charles and she alone knew how little that was. Others were less inclined to believe in her innocence, and she felt that, considering her conduct, she could scarcely blame them for being incredulous. Though she had kept her honour, she had lost her reputation. Unless she were willing now to surrender to the King at last, only one course remained open to her. She must marry. By marriage she could, to a certain extent, vindicate her good name. She herself openly stated afterwards that in the end she had " come to such a pass as to be willing to marry any gentleman of £1500 a year who would have her in honour."[1] It was at this opportune moment that the Duke of Richmond chose to lose his heart to her.

Charles Stuart, 4th Duke of Richmond and 6th Duke of Lennox, was a 4th cousin of the King and a distant kinsman of Frances herself. He was born in London on the 7th March, 1640, the son of George, Lord Aubigny, second son of Esmé, Duke of Lennox, and Lady Catherine Howard, eldest daughter of Theophilus, Earl of Suffolk. Lord Aubigny was killed at Edgehill in 1642, leaving his wife with two children, Charles and Catherine. Lady Aubigny, who had been married again to Sir James Levingstane, died in exile at the Hague in 1650, so that the two children were left parentless at a very early age, and were quietly brought up in the country by relations. Charles I. had created the boy Earl of Lichfield three years after his father's death, and it was by that name that he was known until in 1660 his young cousin, Esmé, Duke of Richmond and Lennox, suddenly died in Paris, where Lichfield himself had also been living for the last two years with his uncle, Lord Aubigny. The King was not the only Charles Stuart, who that year came into great titles and possessions. The new Duke succeeded

[1] Pepys. April 26th, 1667.

La Belle Stuart

to the offices of Great Chamberlain and Hereditary Lord High Admiral of Scotland as well as to the vast Lennox estates and to Cobham Hall, near Gravesend in Kent. In 1660 he married a widow, Elizabeth Cavendish, who had succeeded to the estates of her father, Richard Rogers of Bryanston in Dorset. The marriage gave the young Duke an interest in Dorset, of which county he was made Lord Lieutenant in 1661. About the same time he was created a Knight of the Garter.

The Duke's character, as it has been handed down to posterity, is scarcely engaging. He has been described as a debauchee and a fool, as being sottish in his habits, and as devoid of grace either in mind or body. Gramont declared that in spite of his birth he did not shine at court, and deservedly incurred the contempt of the King and his courtiers. Such unqualified condemnation seems to have been undeserved. That he had serious faults, even vices, cannot be denied, but they have been greatly exaggerated. His worst fault was his addiction to drink, and more especially his failure to confine his excesses in this direction to his leisure hours. On one occasion, indeed, he was severely rebuked by the King for drunken conduct while on a mission to Scotland in 1662 with his stepfather, who had been created Earl of Newburgh at the Restoration. Extravagance was another of his shortcomings. He seems to have been entirely ignorant of the value of money, an unfortunate failing in a man whose large estates had come to him already burdened with debt. Although he was generous, his tradesmen had to suffer for his openhandedness, as their accounts were usually left long unpaid. Racing and betting ran away with a great deal of his money, but even his severest critics admitted that much was applied to worthier purposes, notably the improvement of Cobham Hall. Moreover, during the Dutch wars, he endeavoured to emulate the Elizabethan tradition by fitting out privateers at his own expense and sending them out to prey upon enemy merchantmen. His duties as Lord-Lieutenant of Dorset, a position of great responsibility, especially in time of War, seem to have been discharged actively and well. In short, his faults were no more than those of many other noblemen of his age, his virtues no less, and the reason why his character has been more adversely commented upon is probably that he lacked that polished wit, which at the Court of Charles II. was an ample atonement for almost any shortcomings.

At the time when he fell in love with Frances Stuart he had just lost his second wife, Margaret, daughter of Lawrence Banister and widow of William Lewis. His married life with her had consisted of a series of acrimonious disputes to which only her death could put an end, so that the fact that he was wooing Frances only a few short weeks after his wife's funeral is comprehensible, if not the less indecent.

La Belle Stuart

According to Gramont the Duke's affection for Frances Stuart was inspired less by her charms than by his desire to use her as a means of regaining the King's favour and counteracting the courtiers' ill opinion of him. Gramont obviously bore a grudge against the Duke, and the reason for it is not far to seek; for Richmond had once been a suitor for the hand of Miss Hamilton, whom the Chevalier himself had subsequently married. Gramont's account of this affair may have been biassed, but, even when it is stripped of exaggerations, the bare facts show Richmond's character in a by no means favourable light. The Duke had openly stated that, though he was in love with Miss Hamilton, he would not marry her without a portion. Miss Hamilton was a near relative of the Duke of Ormonde, and her own father had done signal service to the Royalist cause, so the King, unwilling that mere lack of riches should stand in the way of her happiness, offered to provide her with a dowry. But his generosity came too late; for the lady was proud, and declared that, if a man who professed to love her, would not take her for herself alone, he should not have her at all. Moreover she added that she had had leisure to reflect upon the Duke's reputation, and had come to the conclusion that to become a Duchess was not " sufficient recompense for the danger that was to be feared from a brute and a debauchee ! "[1]

[1] Gramont. Memoirs.

Either the Duke learnt a salutary lesson from this ignominious rebuff, or else he put his love for Frances Stuart on a higher plane, for this time there was no talk of the necessity of a dowry.

The Duke was at first too diffident to woo Frances himself, and resolved to approach her through another. He succeeded in attaching to his interests one of the other Maids of Honour, Miss La Garde, and charged her to tell Frances that the Duke of Richmond was dying of love for her, and that the languishing glances he cast at her were a sign that he was ready to marry her as soon as she would consent. Unfortunately history does not relate what response Frances made to these vicarious protestations of love, but she certainly did not keep the Duke so long on tenter-hooks as she had used to do with former admirers. She was now so unnerved by the King's importunities that she was only too eager to accept legitimate advances from anyone so eligible as His Grace of Richmond. But even when she had made up her mind to accept the Duke's proposal her difficulties were by no means at an end. The King's passion for her remained a seemingly insurmountable obstacle between her and her lover. It was difficult to say how His Majesty would take the news of her decision to marry. He could scarcely be expected to give his blessing to the union; but it was questionable whether he would even tolerate her giving herself to anyone else when she had refused herself

FRANCES STUART AS PALLAS
H. Gascar. Goodwood House

to him. Even if he could not actually forbid the marriage, he could do all in his power to prevent it by other means, and, if he chose to do so, his opposition was likely to be formidable.

Worried as Frances was, she was not going to reveal to the world that she had anything to distress her. She continued to attend all the diversions of the Court, as beautiful, as gay, and outwardly as careless as ever. It was during these days that Pepys saw her at the Playhouse. " Great Company," he exclaims, " among others, Mrs. Stewart, very fine, with her locks done up with puffes, as my wife calls them : and several other great ladies had their hair so, though I do not like it ; but my wife do mightily—but it is only because she sees it is the fashion."[1]

Neither Frances nor the Duke deemed it advisable to make any attempt to conceal from the King that there was an understanding between them, and it was plainly intimated to him that they hoped soon to be married. His Majesty, it appears, did not at first offer any objection. Nevertheless they agreed that it would not be politic to flaunt their love in his face, and arranged as far as possible to meet clandestinely. They would have been wiser had they proceeded openly, for these secret trysts proved their undoing. Lady Castlemaine took care to keep her-

Pepys. February 4th, 1667.

self informed of the hours of their meetings, and waited patiently for a suitable opportunity to betray them to the King. Her chance came when one night Frances, on the plea of being tired, had persuaded the King to cut short his evening visit so that she might retire to bed. Having made certain that the Duke of Richmond was with her, Lady Castlemaine hastened to the King's cabinet and informed him that Frances had merely feigned tiredness in order to rid herself of him, and receive the Duke of Richmond in his stead. The King, filled with rage and jealousy, at once returned to Frances's apartments, where he appeared so suddenly that the chambermaids, who were watching at the door, were unable to warn their mistress of his approach. They did their utmost, however, to prevent his entrance, informing him that Miss Stuart had been ill since he left her, but that now she had at last fallen asleep, and it would be cruel to disturb her. But the King was not to be deceived; he flung the protesting maids aside, and pushed his way into the bedchamber. The sight that met his gaze was sufficient to increase his resentment. Frances was lying in bed, and the Duke of Richmond was seated at her pillow, talking to her. The King altogether lost control of his temper and burst forth into such a torrent of threats and abuse that the Duke, deeming that Frances would be more capable than himself of dealing with the enraged monarch, beat a hasty and inglorious retreat.

If the King was furious, Frances was quite as angry, and replied to his invective with bitter recriminations and stinging reproaches. Why, she asked, should she not be allowed to receive visits from the Duke of Richmond, who, at least, came to her with honourable intentions ? Surely it was a matter for herself alone to decide whom she should marry ? If His Majesty thought otherwise, at any rate she knew of nothing that could prevent her from returning to France and retreating into a convent. With this her tears began to flow.

The King could never bear to see a woman cry, nor did his rage altogether blind him to the truth in her reproaches. Little by little his anger died away, and all would perhaps have been well, if Frances, observing that he wavered, had not been so foolish as to abandon her defensive position and attack him in turn. It was not difficult for her to guess whence the betrayal had come, and in her bitterness she could not resist a taunt at the woman who had caused her misfortune. So now, though the King seemed disposed to linger and indulge in a sentimental reconciliation, she begged him to leave her at once ; since otherwise the length of his visit might offend the person at whose suggestion he had come to her apartments. This pointed insinuation threw the King into a worse rage than before : he swore roundly that he hoped he would never set eyes on her again, and, unable to contain himself any longer, he turned on his heel, and abruptly left her apartment.

The events of the next morning showed that this was no fit of temper, but an enduring resentment, for his first action was to give orders that the Duke of Richmond was to leave the Court at once and never dare to come back again. But the Duke, with more wisdom than courage, had not awaited His Majesty's bidding; the early hours of the morning had already seen him well on the way to Cobham Hall.

Frances had had time during her sleepless night to reflect upon the gravity of her mistake, and made up her mind to remedy it as soon as possible. Without any delay she hastened to the Queen's apartments, and, throwing herself at Catherine's feet in tears, she sobbed out the whole story. It was partly for Her Majesty's sake, she declared, that she had incurred her misfortunes, since it was when she had come to realize how her foolish conduct must have caused uneasiness to her mistress, that she had determined to leave the Court, and had listened to the Duke's addresses as the best means of obtaining her wish. Would Her Majesty deign to intercede with the King on her behalf that she might be allowed to marry the Duke and retire from Court, or, if this could not be granted her, might leave be obtained for her to go into a convent? Catherine, who had always been fond of Frances, was deeply touched by her obvious distress. She raised her up and comforted her, promising to help her in any course that she should think it best to pursue.

To approach the Queen and enlist her sympathy was the wisest thing Frances could have done in the circumstances. Catherine was a sensible and a tactful woman, and gave deep consideration to all aspects of the matter. After long reflection she came to the conclusion that the interests of no one concerned would be served by allowing Frances to retire into a convent. Even she herself would suffer, if such a course were adopted, since she knew that she could never hope to retain the inconstant King's volatile affections, and it was preferable that Frances, who had always been devoted to her, should do so rather than the hateful Castlemaine, or some other lady, whose character and disposition were unknown to her. She therefore decided in favour of forwarding the marriage, and by the exercise of great tact succeeded a few days later in patching up a reconciliation between Frances and the King.

When Catherine was urging upon her husband the advisability of forgiving Frances, she had conceivably pointed out to him the impropriety of an open refusal to sanction the marriage; for he henceforth adopted subtler methods in his attempts to break the match. His knowledge that the Duke of Richmond's affairs were in disorder raised a hope that he might be able to wreck the marriage on the rocks of finance. He accordingly sent for the Duke, and, informing him that he would agree to the match provided that a suitable settlement were made on Miss Stuart, he demanded from him a complete and detailed statement of his monetary affairs.[1]

The fact that the marriage was projected was now an open secret,[2] the wedding was expected to take place soon after Easter, and it was even reported that the King had given the Duke of Richmond leave to enlarge his lodgings in the Bowling-Green at Whitehall in order to provide better accommodation for his bride.[3] On March the 19th, Pepys was told " that for certain the match is concluded between the Duke of Richmond and Mrs. Stewart, which I am well enough pleased with : and it is pretty to consider how his quality will allay people's talk ; whereas had a meaner person married her he would for certain have been derided at first dash."

The Duke of Richmond was not taken in by the King's apparent eagerness to help ; he was well aware that His Majesty did not intend the marriage to take place, if he could possibly prevent it, and suspected that he was deliberately protracting the negotiations in the hope of finding some convenient opportunity of breaking them off. So long as reasons for delay

---

[1] Pepys. March 18th, 1667. Burnet. History of His Own Time.
[2] Cal. Stat. Pap. Dom. CXCIV. 91.
[3] Hist. MS. Comm. Report. 12. Ap. vii. MSS. of S. H. Le Fleming at Rydal Hall. p. 46. Newsletter.

could be found, there was always a chance that something unforeseen might occur which would enable him to withdraw his consent, or, better still, might cause Frances or the Duke to abandon the marriage of their own accord. The plan was simple; but much has often been achieved by judicious delay. The Duke was rightly convinced that with every day that passed his chances of marrying Frances were receding, and, being passionately in love with her, determined to leave matters in abeyance no longer. If he were not to be defeated by the King's subtle policy of procrastination, he himself must strike and strike soon. There was little question as to what his action must be; if the King refused or delayed his consent he must marry Frances without it. He did not find it hard to persuade the romantic girl to consent to a runaway match, and their plans were soon laid. One stormy night at the end of March, Frances, wrapped up in a dark cloak, stole from the palace of Whitehall, and made her way across London Bridge to "The Bear at the Bridgefoot," a celebrated and ancient tavern on the Southwark side. Here the Duke awaited her impatiently with a coach in readiness, and after scarcely a moment's delay they dashed off to Cobham Hall.[1]

[1] Pepys. April 3rd, 1667. According to Dr. William Denton writing to Sir Ralph Verney on April the 4th which was a Thursday, "Mrs. Steward was married to Richmond on Satterday last, and in soe doinge they have given ye K some disgust, but what that is I cannot learne." This would make the date of the marriage March 30th. (Original letter at Claydon House).

When the news of the elopement was brought to the King, his rage knew no bounds. He swore that he would never forgive the erring lovers, that he would never consent to see Frances again. His bitterness was increased by the fact that Frances had left behind her all the jewels he had given her, with instructions that they were to be returned to him.[1] They consisted of a pearl necklace worth some £1100, which he had given her when she first came to Court, and one or two other less considerable pieces of jewelry, which he had pressed upon her when he " had hopes to have obtained some courtesy of her."

According to the custom of the time it was perfectly allowable for a young girl to receive valuable presents from admirers, without any particular significance being attached to her acceptance. Even Frances, who had never been avaricious, and had never sought those gifts which had been so lavishly distributed among other ladies at Court, seems to have amassed some wonderful jewels. The Duke of York, who had been her valentine one year, had given her a jewel valued at £800, and only a month or so back she had received a ring worth £300 from Lord Mandeville,[2] her valentine of this year. John Evelyn told Pepys that he believed " she may be worth in jewells about £6000, and that is all she

---

[1] Pepys. April 26th, 1667.
[2] Robert Montagu, Viscount Mandeville, son of the Lord Chamberlain, the Earl of Manchester.

hath in the world; and a worthy woman; and in this hath done as great an act of honour as ever was done by woman."[1]

Evelyn had heard Frances's own version of the facts of the marriage from a nobleman of sober character and unimpeachable veracity, to whom she had told everything in her desire to justify her conduct. She said that she had at last realized " that she could not longer continue at Court without prostituting herself to the King, whom she had so long kept off, though he had liberty more than any other had, or he ought to have, as to dalliance! She told this lord that she had reflected upon the occasion she had given the world to think her a bad woman, and that she had no way but to marry and leave the Court, rather in this way of discontent than otherwise, that the world might see that she sought not anything but her honour; and that she will never come to live at Court more than when she comes to town to kiss the Queen her mistress's hand." Evelyn himself knew Frances well, and believed her " up to her leaving the Court to be as virtuous as any woman in the world." Whatever other people may have thought or said about her, it was something to have the good opinion of the level-headed and sober-minded John Evelyn. At any rate his evident belief in Frances Stuart's virtue and

[1] Pepys. April 26th, 1667.

sincerity sufficed to convert Pepys from his previous opinion of her morals. Nor was Evelyn alone in his opinion, for the story was to be heard from other quarters. " Pierce told us the story how, in good earnest, the King is offended with the Duke of Richmond's marrying, and Mrs. Stewart's sending the King his jewels again. As he tells it, it is the noblest romance, and example of a brave lady that ever I read in my life."[1]

The Duke and Duchess of Richmond seem at first to have hoped that now their marriage was an accomplished fact the King might be willing to let bygones be bygones, and receive them again into favour. Accordingly on April the 3rd, only a few days after their marriage, they returned to London and went to the lodgings of Frances's mother in Somerset House, where they remained in strict privacy until they could discover what sort of reception they would experience at Court. But it soon became obvious that the fatted calf would not be slain in their honour. Finding that His Majesty's displeasure was really unfeigned, they deemed it wisest to retire again to Cobham Hall.[2]

The marriage of La Belle Stuart with the Duke of Richmond was to have the most far-reaching consequences in that it was the occasion of the fall of

[1] Pepys. April 16th, 1667.
[2] Hist. MSS. Comm. Report 12 Ap. vii. ' MSS. of S. H. Le Fleming at Rydall Hall.' p. 46. Newsletter.

Lord Chancellor Clarendon, who had for so long guided the country's destinies. His enemies, always on the watch for an opportunity to strike him down, saw that they could do so now, if they could only successfully impute to him the blame for this marriage. The Chancellor's enemies were many and powerful, and were admirably led by those whose hatred for him arose from a desire to take his place. In their efforts to ruin him they were well assured of popular support, since Clarendon was cordially detested by the lower classes, in whose minds he was always associated with the sale of Dunkirk to the French. By his whole-hearted support of the Church of England he had alienated both Papist and Dissenter ; and, in his desire to stabilize the royal power by conciliating all political parties in the State, he had earned the implacable hatred of the Old Cavaliers, who considered that their unremitting loyalty to the King should have entitled them to enjoy all offices under the new government, to the exclusion of others who had been less loyal. Moreover, the ideal for which he had always striven—constitutional monarchy based on a perfect balance between the powers of Crown and Parliament—was congenial to neither party. The King, more especially, had chafed under the restraints thereby imposed upon him by the Chancellor, and had bitterly resented Clarendon's refusal,at the beginning of his reign, to allow an enthusiastic and subservient

Parliament to settle such a revenue upon him as would have for the future made him altogether independent of Parliaments, and enabled him to institute an autocracy. In addition to these purely political grievances the King also harboured resentment against Clarendon for personal reasons connected with his constant gouty ill-temper, and even more with his frequent efforts to persuade His Majesty to lead a more moral life. The King's feelings were well known to Clarendon's enemies, who were convinced that he was in his heart eager to dismiss the Chancellor, and that he was restrained only by a certain sense of gratitude for the great services, which this old and tried servant had rendered both to his father and to himself, and also by his reluctance to take a step so momentous that it would be bound to shock him from his state of unconcerned laziness. Yet the embers of his resentment smouldered on, and only a spark was needed to make them burst into flame. Arlington and his friends, in alliance with Lady Castlemaine, whose enmity for the Chancellor was at least understandable, since he had never disguised his dislike for her, and had avowedly been as eager for her dismissal as she was for his, had worked unceasingly to exasperate the King's impatience at Clarendon's domination. Their tongues were never free from insinuations and calumnies, and they were ably assisted by the 'comical and licentious persons of both sexes,' whom the rigid Clarendon had ever been rather too apt to frown upon and rebuke. His sincere conviction that their presence at Court was a contaminating influence no doubt justified his severity, but it did not contribute to his popularity. The Courtiers hated him for the rectitude of his morals and the solemnity of his manner, and would jeer at the King for allowing the Chancellor to assume a dictatorial manner even with him. " There goes your Schoolmaster ! " they would say to the King mockingly as Clarendon passed by.

Chief among the scoffers was the Duke of Buckingham, who was now one of the Chancellor's most unrelenting enemies. His volatile temperament made his conduct so erratic that he was by turns in and out of the King's favour like a jack-in-the-box, and it had been found possible to persuade him that the Chancellor was responsible for the rigour with which one of his recent misdemeanours had been punished. His talent for insidious mockery was now bent to the task of lowering Clarendon in the King's estimation. He used to mimic him in the royal presence, strutting along in a pompous and stately fashion with a pair of bellows representing the purse, and one Colonel Titus walking gravely before him with a fire-shovel on his shoulder for the mace.[1] It was by buffoonery such as this, and by a multitude of hints, insinuations,

[1] Echard's History.

and sarcasms, calculated by cumulative effect to produce irritation with and contempt for the person upon whom all this ridicule was poured, that the King's scruples had gradually been removed. The slightest circumstance would now induce him to take the final step.

The King's fury at Frances Stuart's marriage was a god-send to the Chancellor's enemies. The rumour was spread abroad that the marriage had been arranged by Clarendon. It was said that the Chancellor, fearing that Charles had become so infatuated with Frances Stuart, that, if he failed to obtain her in any other way, he might be tempted to divorce the Queen and marry her, and believing that the political consequences of such a course would be disastrous both for the King and for the country, had determined to guard against such a possibility by furthering her marriage to the Duke of Richmond. This was at least crediting Clarendon with disinterested and patriotic motives; but certain of his enemies were not averse to inventing more scandalous accusations. It began to be whispered at Court that a more flagitious motive lay behind the Chancellor's eagerness to promote the Richmond marriage. His daughter was Duchess of York, and, if the King should die childless, his grandchildren would eventually succeed to the Crown. Did not these circumstances provide a feasible explanation of the Chancellor's machinations? Pepys heard the odious calumny from Sir William Batten.[1] It also came to the ears of Bishop Burnet, who repeats it, though with the qualification "whether true or false I cannot tell." He says that he was told that the King ordered Clarendon to examine the Duke of Richmond's estate in order to find some justification for breaking off the match with Frances Stuart, and that His Majesty was afterwards informed that Clarendon had played him false, and had gone to Frances and told her that, though it was true that the Duke's finances were at present involved, he was so nearly related to the Royal House that the King for his own honour could never allow him to be ruined. For this reason she should consider well before she rejected the addresses of so exalted a nobleman. "This was carried to the King, as a design he had that the crown might descend to his own grandchildren; and that he was afraid lest strange methods should be taken to get rid of the Queen, and to make way for her."

Clarendon was even openly accused of having arranged the King's marriage with Catherine in the furtherance of his subtle plots for the exaltation of his own descendants. The idea that he had deliberately foisted on Charles a Queen, whom he knew to be incapable of bearing children, was sedulously fostered. A lampoon, written by some scurrilous

[1] Pepys. July 17th, 1667.

wit with a disposition for doggerel, had gone the rounds at Court.

> " God bless Queen Kate
> Our sovereign's mate,
> Of the royal house of Lisbon.
> But the devil take Hyde
> And the bishop beside
> Who made her bone of his bone."

The popularity of the sentiment was held to be sufficient excuse for the execrable rhyme. Equally feeble verse was produced by the populace, who painted a gibbet on the gates of Clarendon House, and scrawled beneath it : " Three sights to be seen : Dunkirk, Tangier, and a barren Queen." Charles himself knew well enough that there was no foundation for this charge. Clarendon had all along favoured a Protestant marriage ; the King himself had deliberately chosen Catherine at the instigation of Louis XIV. and contrary to the advice of the Chancellor, who had merely acquiesced in the Portuguese marriage when he saw that Charles would not entertain the idea of a Protestant alliance. Not that Charles would have borne the Chancellor any malice had he arranged the marriage, for, though he regretted his wife's childlessness, he was deeply devoted to her. Any idea that the King ever projected divorcing the Queen may be categorically rejected. The talk of divorce, of which there certainly was much towards the end of this year, arose from the desires of others to see her divorced from him, and not from the King himself. Charles would never listen to such suggestions from the few, who, like Buckingham, were bold enough to approach him on the subject. It is scarcely likely, therefore, that there is any truth in the story that the King asked Archbishop Sheldon whether the Church would allow of a divorce when both parties were consenting and one of them lay under a natural incapacity of having children. Sheldon is supposed to have asked for time to consider the question, and had permission to do so under a solemn promise of secrecy. The Archbishop of Canterbury promptly broke his oath and revealed to the Chancellor that the King designed to divorce the Queen in order to marry Frances Stuart. Clarendon then arranged the Richmond marriage as an effective means of preventing the divorce.[1]

It is almost incredible that such accusations as these, levelled by unprincipled persons such as Buckingham and Lady Castlemaine against men of the character of Clarendon and Sheldon, should be held sufficient to prove that Clarendon was responsible for the marriage. Yet Charles affected to believe them, and there can be no doubt that they

---

[1] Burnet's "History of His Own Time" and Lord Dartmouth's note on this passage.

were the cause of his making up his mind at last to dismiss the Chancellor.

At first the King may have sincerely believed what he had been told; for an incident which occurred the morning after the elopement might have given colour to his suspicions. As he came from Frances's empty lodgings, furious at her departure, he met the Chancellor's son, Lord Cornbury, who, knowing nothing of the elopement, and having an appointment with Frances, was about to enter. The King at once suspected that Cornbury had been an accomplice in the plot, and " spoke to him as one in a rage that forgot all decency, and for some time would not hear Lord Cornbury speak in his own defence." By the afternoon the King had cooled down sufficiently to listen to and accept Cornbury's explanations, but a suspicion still lingered in his mind.[1]

Clarendon could not disguise from himself during the ensuing months that his doom was about to be sealed, for the King treated him with growing disfavour. Yet he was slow to believe that Charles could really credit what he himself regarded as preposterous allegations made by Lady Castlemaine and others of his enemies. Shortly after the marriage one of his friends, a trustworthy person, whom he himself describes as " a person of honour who knew the truth of it," came and informed him " that some

---

[1] Burnet.

persons had persuaded the King that the Chancellor had a principal hand in the marriage of the Duke of Richmond, with which his majesty was offended in the highest degree: and that the lord Berkley had reported it with all confidence."

Clarendon, who knew Berkley for a secret enemy in spite of his professions of friendship, had at once taxed him with what he was reported to have said; but Berkley had flatly denied that he had said any such thing. The Chancellor then went to the King himself, and asked him outright whether any such story had been told him, for there was no truth in it. The King had answered with some dryness that "no such thing had been told to him." Charles was probably ashamed of his suspicions, and did not care to admit them, but Clarendon was even now assured that this was the reason for the King's coldness to him, coupled with the ill-temper which he showed when he and the King differed in opinion. In these circumstances he thought fit to write a long letter to the King.[1]

May it please your Majesty

I am so broken under the daily insupportable instances of your Majesty's terrible displeasure, that I know not what to do, hardly what to wish. The crimes which are objected against me, how

[1] Clarendon. Continuation. 1181.

passionately soever pursued, and with circumstances very unusual, do not in the least degree fright me. God knows I am innocent in every particular as I ought to be ; and I hope your Majesty knows enough of me to believe that I had never a violent appetite for money, that could corrupt me. But alas ! your Majesty's declared anger and indignation deprives me of the comfort and support even of my own innocence, and exposes me to the rage and fury of those who have some excuse for being my enemies ; whom I have sometimes displeased, when (and only then) your Majesty believed them not to be your friends. I hope they may be changed ; I am sure I am not ; but have the same duty, passion, and affection for you, that I had when you thought it most unquestionable, and which was and is as great as ever man had for any mortal creature. I should die in peace (and truly I do heartily wish that God Almighty would free you from further trouble by taking me to himself) if I could know or guess at the ground of your displeasure, which I am sure must proceed from your believing that I have said or done somewhat I have neither said or done. If it be for anything my Lord Berkley hath reported, which I know he hath said to many, though being charged with it by me he did as positively disclaim it ; I am as innocent in that whole affair, and gave no more advice or countenance in it, than the child that is (not) born : which your majesty seemed once to believe, when I took notice to you of the report, and when you considered how totally I was a stranger to the persons mentioned, to either of whom I never spake word, or received message from either in my life. And this I protest to your majesty is true, as I have hope in heaven : and that I have never wilfully offended your majesty in my life, and do upon my knees beg your pardon for any over-bold or saucy expressions I have ever used to you ; which, being a natural disease in old servants who have received too much countenance, I am sure have always proceeded from the zeal and warmth of the most sincere affection and duty.

I hope your majesty believes, that the sharp chastisement I have received from the best-natured and most bountiful master in the world, and whose kindness alone made my condition these many years supportable, hath enough mortified me as to this world ; and that I have not the presumption or the madness to imagine or desire ever to be admitted to any employment or trust again. But I do most humbly beseech your majesty, by the memory of your father, who recommended me to you with some testimony, and by your own gracious reflection upon some one service I may have performed in my life, that hath been acceptable to you ; that you will by your royal power and interposition put a stop to this severe prosecution against me, and that my concernment may give no longer interruption to the great affairs of the kingdom; but that I may spend the small remainder of my life, which cannot hold long, in some parts beyond the seas, never to return; where I will pray for your majesty, and never suffer the least diminution in the duty and obedience of,

  May it please your majesty,
   Your Majesty's
    Most humble and most
     Obedient subject and servant,
      Clarendon.

This letter Clarendon entrusted to his friend, the Lord Keeper, to deliver to the King. Charles read it through, and merely remarking " that there was somewhat in it that he did not understand, but that he wondered that the Chancellor did not withdraw himself," stretched the letter towards a lighted candle that was on the table, and held it in the flame till it was consumed.[1] The Lord Keeper saw that the King's mind was irrevocably made up, and returned to the Chancellor with the news that his mission had failed and that only flight could save him from the fury of his enemies.

[1] The existing copy of this letter is in the handwriting of Lawrence, Earl of Rochester, Clarendon's second son.

La Belle Stuart

His spirit broken by the King's failure to support him, the Chancellor at last succumbed to the entreaties of his friends, and made his escape to France. Thus fell the great Earl of Clarendon, the victim of his enemies' malice and his King's ingratitude. Considering his unpopularity it is a matter for wonder that he should have been able for so long to withstand the attacks made upon him. He had always prided himself upon his refusal to conciliate the circle of libertines which surrounded the King; but it was to his failure to do so that he owed his downfall. It was the Court that had overwhelmed him in the end, just as it had brought many other great men to ruin.

> By thee[1] fell Wolsey and false Clarendon,
> Abandon'd by their kings, but here undone:
> Both overwhelm'd for daring to remove,
> Or stem the torrent of their master's love.
> The one fair Bullen to his prince deny'd
> The other made lov'd Stuart Richmond's bride
> And with the Royal blood for ever mingled Hide.

But all the same so great had been his power that it had taken even such consummate intriguers as Arlington, Buckingham, Sir William Coventry, and Lady Castlemaine years of ceaseless plotting to

---

[1] Lines referring to the Court and attributed to Lord S(ackville), Miscellaneous Works of the Earl of Roscommon, etc., 1709.

compass his destruction. Such a patient and remorseless campaign could not have failed to succeed in its object sooner or later, even if the Richmond marriage had not taken place, but it was this that had given it its final impetus, and it was by emphasizing Clarendon's responsibility in the matter that his enemies had been able to push their vindictiveness to its uttermost limit, and compass the Chancellor's entire disgrace. There is something peculiarly appropriate to the time in the thought that the dismissal of England's strongest statesman, the King's most honest and faithful public servant, was finally decided upon, because he was supposed to have thwarted His Majesty's amorous designs upon a young and frivolous lady of the Queen's household.

Note.—The foregoing account of the Richmond marriage is founded chiefly on Pepys's diary, Echard's History, Gramont's Memoirs, Burnet's History of His Own Time, and Clarendon's "Continuation" of his "Life." Unfortunately the usual French evidence is not available, for after the failure of the "célèbre ambassade extraordinaire" diplomatic relations between England and France were broken off. There are no ambassadors' despatches between December 13th, 1666, and August 11th, 1667. A still greater misfortune is the absence, for the same reason, of letters from Charles to his sister between those dated October 18th, 1666 and July 27th, 1667.

CHAPTER VI

Frances missed by the Court—Lord St. Alban's letter to the Duke—Charles refuses his forgiveness—The Duke and Duchess at Cobham Hall—Rumour that an heir is expected—The Duke called away to Dorset—Frances writes to him from Cobham—Peace with Holland—Frances Stuart as Britannia on the Medals—Waller's poem—Madame intercedes for Frances—The King rejects her overtures—The Richmonds contemplate retiring to France—Letter from Henry Coventry—Frances at Somerset House—Possibility of a reconciliation discussed—The King holds back—Frances ill with smallpox—Charles hesitates no longer—Lady Castlemaine set by—The King climbs over a garden-gate—Frances appointed a Lady of the Bed-chamber—The Duke and Duchess of Richmond move to Whitehall—Pepys makes the Duke's acquaintance, but fails to meet the Duchess.

The departure of Frances Stuart from the Court was regretted by all save those few who, like Lady Castlemaine, felt securer in their own charms now that they were no longer overshadowed by her beauty. Her gay and charming presence was sadly missed by the laughter-loving crowd, which had been wont every evening to throng her apartments, and it was felt that her departure had left a blank that no one else could fill. Sir Charles Lyttelton absent with the fleet at Harwich, wrote to his friend

Christopher Hatton anxiously asking to be told what had become of her, and " where those vacant howers are spent now that used to be pass'd away at her chamber."[1] But the King's wrath had fallen upon her; the courtiers, not venturing to protest openly, could only lament her departure in secret. The Queen-Mother, who had always stood by Frances, and might have pleaded for her now, was away in Paris. She probably sympathized with the young lovers, for the Earl of St. Alban's, her chief confidant and adviser—some say her husband—wrote to the Duke of Richmond expressing his approval of the step he had taken. " I take it for great honor in a season soe likely to take up all your thoughts that you have found leisure for the account you have bin pleased to give me of your self, and of my own concearnments. I beseeche your grace to beleeve that in order to the first I take the part I ought to doe not onely in reference to my respects to you but by the obligations of the honor I have to be related to the person you have chosen, and that I wish you both all sorts of felicity."[2]

[1] Hatton Correspondence I. 52.
[2] B.M. Add MSS. 21947 f.55. Extensive research has so far failed to reveal the relationship between Lord St. Alban's and Frances Stuart, alluded to in this letter. There does not appear to have been any kinship between the Jermyns and the Stuarts of Blantyre, so that in all probability the connection was through the family of the Hon. Mrs. Walter Stuart, whose maiden name has never been discovered.

The King's anger with Frances is at least understandable; for, though she had a perfect right to marry the Duke of Richmond, if she wished, she had done it in a way that showed very little regard for His Majesty's feelings. It is true that his advances to her had not been of a very honourable nature, and there was no reason why she should have responded to them, but, if she was from the very beginning firmly resolved never to become the King's mistress, she ought to have made it quite clear to him that it was useless to persist. Instead she had always deliberately given him the impression that he might overcome her reluctance in the end, and had repelled his advances in such a manner as not to deprive him of all hope. So now, when he realized that from the very first this artful minx had been deceiving him, it is little to be wondered at that he felt deeply aggrieved, and swore roundly that he would never forgive her or her husband, and would never suffer them to come to Court again.

For the time being this prohibition failed to perturb the Duke and Duchess of Richmond. Utterly engrossed one with the other they found their exile sweet. Nor could a more wonderful place be found for a honeymoon than Cobham Hall in spring-time. The Duke had always loved this home of his, and had already spent a great part of his fortune in additions to the stately red brick house with its octagonal turrets and quaint clusters of Tudor chimneys. Frances too was quick to fall under the spell of the place, and she and her husband applied themselves with ardour to the agreeable task of re-decorating the apartments they intended to occupy. With matters of such importance to occupy their minds they entirely forgot their sovereign's rage, and gave no thought to the difficulties they were laying up for themselves in the future.

Early in June a rumour that the Duke and Duchess of Richmond were expecting an heir reached the Duke's estates in Scotland. The enthusiasm was enormous, and so fervent was the loyalty of the ducal tenants that everyone took it for granted that the new-comer would be a boy. Richmond's agent in Scotland wrote to him from Edinburgh on June the 8th:

" I am afrayd the newes of her Grace's being with child will make all your Grace's vassals mad; some of them have come to me allmost 100 miles only to be informed of the certainty. It is looked upon here as no small miracle to heare soe great brutes as they be so heartily zealous for both your Graces and the young Lord Darnley, and I hope your Grace will be easily perswaded that it hath extremely added to the devotion of your Grace's most humble obedient and faithful servant, J. Boreman."[1]

Although there is no other evidence that the

---

[1] B.M. Add MSS. 21,947 f. 67.

COBHAM HALL. KENT

Duchess was ever in such a condition, it seems improbable that Boreman would have dared to write in such plain terms to the Duke, if he had not received official intimation of the approaching event. At any rate the high hopes were destined to be disappointed, for, sad to relate, there was to be no little Lord Darnley, nor even a little Lady Frances to make the Scottish vassals still more heartily zealous for the House of Lennox.

The Duke and Duchess were not to be left for long undisturbed in the enjoyment of their new-found happiness. Official duties called the Duke away from Cobham. The death of Felipe IV. of Spain had brought the question of the Spanish Netherlands once more into prominence. His heir, Carlos II., was not expected to live long, and France must therefore be prepared at any moment to assert her claims. Louis XIV. considered that in the circumstances this war with England was nothing more than a waste of energy. His purpose had been served, as both England and Holland had been considerably weakened by the constant drain on their resources. Now, therefore, he renewed his efforts for peace, and this time with more success, seeing that his intentions were sincere. England was ready enough for peace, though the Dutch were less eager, because they already foresaw that peace between England and France would merely be a first step to an alliance between them. Louis XIV., however, was powerful enough to compel their acquiescence, and as a result of his efforts representatives of all the powers met at Breda to negotiate a peace. But, although nearly every important point was quickly settled, the English Commissioners, Lord Holles and Henry Coventry, chose to assume a rigid and uncompromising attitude in regard to various lesser matters. Their refusal to come to terms exasperated the Dutch to such a pitch that they determined there was nothing for it but to force England's hand by some bold stroke. This course was all the more congenial to them since they were wishful, before peace was declared, to take an adequate revenge for the burning of Schelling by the English fleet in the preceding year. In the month of June, therefore, a Dutch fleet sailed up the Medway and wrought havoc among the shipping lying there. The unexpectedness of the attack and the ease with which the enemy had accomplished their purpose threw the whole country into consternation, and it was freely rumoured that a Dutch invasion might be expected at any moment. On a report that the Dutch fleet was sailing off the Dorset Coast, the Duke of Richmond, as Lord Lieutenant, received orders to go down and put his county into a posture to resist attack. He proceeded west on the evening of June the 27th.[1] Frances remained at home. To be left

---

[1] B.M. Add MSS. 23,127 f. 74.

La Belle Stuart

alone in a house as big as Cobham Hall to cope with builders and decorators is surely a severe test of the intelligence and common sense of any young woman, especially when she can have had little experience of the notorious ways of such people. But the young Duchess seems to have acquitted herself admirably of the task, though she found it sufficiently difficult, as she herself told the Duke : [1]

Cobham the 11 of july.

My dearest Lord,

Yesterday I reseved a letter from you ; it is the second since you arrived at Dorchester, and for which I give you many thankes, becasse it has eaysed me of a great delle of care and trobel that I had, fearing you were not well. Oh, my dearest, if you love me, have a care of your selfe, for longer then you are in health I cannot be in rest. I will not fayle to send to Mr. Freeman about what you desiered. This day Captain Jonson came heyther to bring me news of the Francis.[2] I will not give you the trobel of a duble relation conserning her ; and I beleve in this inclosed hee has don it at full. Prince Rupert has bin thisse too dayes in the ile of Sheppay to fortify Sheerness, which the Citty of London has undertaken to do for Ten Thousand pound, and the King gives it them ; so that Sir

---

[1] B.M. Add MSS. 21,947. f. 55.   [2] The Duke's yacht.

Johe Robinson[1] is now thayr to see what materialls the prince will comand for that purpos ; my Lord Gorge came yesterday from Sheerness and by him the prince did desier me to send him a buck. I gave order imediatly to have an out Layen Deere[2] hunted : which was done this morning, but they could not gitt any, so that I think tis best to have one shotte. I hope before this comes to your hands you will have leve to come home again, for I longe extreemly to see my Dere Lord in whom consists all my hapyness. I wonder you have not reseved your powder, for I sent it by Dicke Rogers : the snuffers and pan I have again, for I suspected you had given them to have the armes changed, and I sent to Mr. Tilson for them. I writ you word long since that Miller was returned, but he beeing wanting 6 days I thought he was run away : upon which I hyered the other painter you mention to paint the Bed-chamber. It is now almost done and lickwis all that apartment, but the Alcove cannot possibly be done in too months, which maid me advis you not to lett them go about it this sumer. If you did but know how hard it is to gitt workmen at this time, and how laysey thosse are which are here, I am sure you woulld be

---

[1] Lord Lieutenant of the Tower and sometime Lord Mayor of London.

[2] An " Outlier " is a deer that has escaped from the bounds of the enclosure within which the herd is confined.

of my opinion. I have tolld Tempel that you have ordered him money, but if he dos not make more hast then he has done yet I will not pay it him so sone, for in ernest he is a very iddel felow. The next weeke Flexney[1] shall buy some deall bordes, for then thayer will want some. Mr. Payne[2] is at his own house, but will be here againe in Too or three dayes ; then I am confident he will tell you, as I do, that tis the hardest thinge in nature now to gitt workmen. I have given order to have the Court inclossed with all speed immaginabel—and thayer are a great many payls allredy cutt ; but now wee cannot have sawyers to do the rest. I hope we shall eare long : pray excues this tedious letter and continue your kindnesse to her that is

>your most affectionat
>wife and servant
>F. Richmond & Lenox.

I have not had any newes yet from Coll Titus ; nor from the Oring Tree.

My Ld. Gorge, my mother, and my sister all present thayer most humbel servis to you, soe dose Mr. L' Omell with all respect immaginabel. Since I writ thiss I reseved one from you in which I find I am still the hapyest wouman that ever was borne in haveing the hart of my dearest Lord

---

[1] [2] In a list of the Duke's servants (B.M. Add MSS. 21, 951 f. 7) are included Roger Payne, Steward, £50 per annum, and Henry fflaxney, Wardroom keeper, £15.

and the only joy of my life ; which I will rather
chusse to dy than lousse. I will not writ you the
Artikels of peace which are agreed upon becasse
I beleve you have heard them allredy. Ambassador Conventry is gone this morning post to
Holland soe as that it is to lait to writ to my Lord
Cornbury to speake to him.[1] I hope you will now
(that wee have peace) come back quickly and do
your own buissenesse, becasse you understand it
better than anyone ellse, though in the mean time
if you have any commands for me, lett me know
them, and I will, I assure you, to se them executed
to the best of my power. I have sent my letters
to Monsieur Courtin and my cossen Howard ten
dayes ago. Yesterday I reseved this inclossed
from my Lord St. Albans, and am very sory to
find the house is not at his disposall ; becase I
fere Sir Hary, if it be his, will kepe it for him selfe
now he is maryed. I think your best way were
to writ immedeately to him about it ; becasse you
did mention it to him once before you went to
Dorsetshir, and he, I remember, ansered you that
if it were in his power to lett, it should be at your
servis.

Mr. Ratten has not bin here since I reseved

---

[1] Probably in regard to the matter of Aubigny, see postea.
The Duchess herself wrote to Coventry about it on the 12th of
July. His reply dated August 5th n.s. is in the Marquess of
Bath's collection at Longleat.

your orders to have the measer of the stones for coping sent you ; when he comes I will not fayl to do it."

The affection for her husband obviously displayed by Frances in this letter shows that Charles had not been mistaken in believing that her marriage would prove an end to all his hopes. If Frances had not loved Richmond and intended to be faithful to him the King would have been the last to resent the marriage ; since it was usual for royal mistresses to go through the formality of marriage with some luckless fellow, it being for some reason considered less reprehensible for a monarch to engage in a love-affair with a married woman than with a girl whose heart was her own and on whose favours no one had a claim.

Frances was showing how admirably she could adapt herself to her circumstances ; it is amusing to find the butterfly of a few months since now writing solemnly of paint and coping-stones, and showing exemplary firmness and decision in her dealings with recalcitrant workmen. But though she could be serious when occasion arose, her natural gaiety had not left her, and she was to show later on that she could be as joyous and as high-spirited as ever.

The shock of the Medway disaster had induced the English envoys at Breda to recede from their untenable position, and the peace was now to all intents and purposes accomplished. When Coventry came over from Holland with the draft of a treaty, which was to be signed if both parties agreed to it, the King gave out openly that the peace had been concluded, even though it was not yet ratified. Several medals were struck to celebrate the naval victories during the Dutch War, and to commemorate the peace which ended it. The King's head was placed on the obverse, and on the reverse it was decided to place the figure of Britannia contemplating her navies sailing on the ocean. That which had originally been designed as a symbol of Britain's subjection was now to be adopted as the emblem of her triumphs. A similar figure representing Rome seated on the shores of Britain had originally appeared on the coins of Claudius after his conquest of the island, but now, though the rock still represented the shores of Britain, Britannia herself was to be enthroned thereon. By express command of His Majesty, Frances Stuart had sat to the engraver Roettier for the figure of Britannia, and, although she had since fallen from favour, the design was not altered. One of the designs was afterwards adapted as the reverse for the copper coinage and except for minor changes has remained essentially the same to this day.[1]

[1] Cf. E. Heron-Allen F.R.S. "Selsey Bill, Historic and Prehistoric," p. 339 and Plate LII, wherein the process of evolution is illustrated.

There is no lack of contemporary evidence to show that Frances Stuart was actually the model for Britannia. John Evelyn considered the likeness excellent[1]: "Monsieur Roti (Graver to his late Majesty Charles II). so accurately express'd the countenance of the Duchess of R—— in the Head of Britannia, in the reverse of some of our Coin, and especially in a Medal, as one may easily, and almost at first sight, know it to be her Grace: And tho' in smallest copper, both for the Persons represented, and performance of the Artist such as may justly stand in competition with the Antient Masters:"

Pepys also, as usual, can bear testimony[2]: very little seems to have escaped his all-pervading curiosity! "At my goldsmith's did observe the King's new medall, where, in little, there is Mrs. Stewart's face as well done as ever I saw anything in my whole life, I think: and a pretty thing it is, that he should choose her face to represent Britannia by."

Jan Roettier, the eldest of several brothers, all engravers to Charles II., seems to have been the engraver of these medals.[3] There appears to be no warrant for Horace Walpole's assertion that the designer was a younger brother, Philippe, who "became so passionately enamoured of Miss Stewart

[1] John Evelyn "Numismata" p. 27.
[2] Pepys. February 25th, 1667.
[3] Ex Inf. Department of Coins and Medals, B.M.

while she sat to him, as nearly to lose his senses."[1] The bare fact that, in addition to the medals on which Frances was represented as Britannia, several portrait-medals of her are in existence is scarcely sufficient justification for assuming that the engraver was in love with his model. Medals were also struck of other famous ladies of the period, including Lady Castlemaine and Louise de Keroualle, Duchess of Portsmouth.

With the object of further expressing England's claim to the "Dominion of the Seas," appropriate mottoes were placed on the medals.[2] Some bore the legend "Favente Deo," others, "Quatuor Maria Vindico." These last words were popularly attributed to the Saxon King, Edgar, who, having conquered seven minor kings, and made the island of Britain into a single kingdom, sailed round it once a year with a thousand ships.[3]

On the occasion when the Dutch sailed up the Medway, the satirist, Andrew Marvell, waxed most sarcastic about England's boast to rule the four seas.

[4]" The Court in Farthering yet it self does please,
(And female Stewart there rules the four Seas,)
But fate does still accumulate our woes,
And Richmond her commands, as Ruyter those."

[1] Walpole. "Anecdotes of Painting."

[2] For further information concerning these medals see Hawkin's "Medallic Illustrations of British History."

[3] C.A. 89 f. 150 Ruvigny to Louis XIV. Oct. 10th, 1667.

[4] Andrew Marvell. "Last Instructions to a Painter about the Dutch Wars, 1667." Poems on Affairs of State I. 73.

MEDALS BY JAN ROETTIER

Fig. 1. The Duchess of Richmond
Fig. 2. Obverse of a Peace of Breda medal, 1667
Fig. 3. Reverse of Fig. 2. The Duchess of Richmond as Britannia
Fig. 4. (in centre) The Duchess of Richmond
Fig. 5. Rejected design for obverse of a Naval Victories Medal

La Belle Stuart

The satire rather loses its sting when it is known that the Duchess of Richmond, far from triumphing over the Court at Whitehall, was on the other hand practically an exile at Cobham. More in accordance with the true circumstances, if the interpretation put upon it be allowable,[1] is Edmund Waller's epigram "Upon the Golden Medal," wherein he compliments the Duchess upon the invulnerability of her virtue.

> "Our guard upon the royal side!
> On the reverse our beauty's pride!
> Here we discern the frown and smile;
> The force and glory of our isle.
> In the rich medal, both so like
> Immortals stand, it seems antique;
> Carv'd by some master, when the bold
> Greeks made their Jove descend in gold;
>
> And Danae wond'ring at that show'r
> Which falling storm'd her brazen tow'r
> Britannia there the fort in vain
> Had battr'd been with golden rain;
> Thunder itself had fail'd to pass;
> Virtue's a stronger guard than brass."

---

[1] This theory is advanced by Fenton in his edition of Waller's works, 1729. The author of the "The Medallic Illustrations of British History," who quotes only the first two lines, suggests that the golden medal was one which portrayed the King on the obverse and the Queen on the reverse. But since there is no medal on which the Queen was habited as Britannia, the rest of the poem would be pointless.

As soon as the young Duchess of Orleans was able to resume her interrupted correspondence with Charles II. she took up the cause of Frances Stuart, and wrote to the King begging him to take her into favour again. But Charles considered that Frances had acted maliciously towards him, and that was a fault he could not bring himself to forgive. As he had written to Madame some years before (July 1664) he was " one of those Bigotts who thinke that malice is a much greater sinn than a poor frailety of nature." He had been too much hurt in his pride to be willing to regard Frances's escapade as due to a frailty of nature, and to the Duchess's appeal he returned a firm refusal.

" I do assure you that I am very much troubled that I cannot in everything give you that satisfaction I could wish, especially in this businesse of the duchesse of Richmond, wherein you may think me ill natured. But, if you consider how hard a thing tis to swallow an injury done by a person I had so much [1]tendernesse for you will in some degree excuse the resentement I use towards her. You know my good nature enough to beleeve that I could not be so severe if I had not great provocation, and I assure you her carriage towards me has been as bad as breach of friendship

---

[1] Here is an " l " deleted. The King was evidently about to write " love," but thought better of it.

and faith can make it. Therefore I hope you will pardon me if I cannot so soon forgett an injury which went so neere my hart."[1]

Charles was not by nature an unforgiving man; the wound must have been deep for him to have written thus months after it had been inflicted. It is not known whether the Duchess of Orleans ventured to approach him again after this very definite refusal, or whether anyone else attempted to succeed where she had failed. At any rate the King remained inexorable; so much so indeed that at one time the Duke and Duchess are believed to have thought of leaving England for good and taking up their abode permanently in France, where the Duke of Richmond was hereditary Duke of Aubigny, an estate in Berri, which had been raised to a ducal fief in 1422 by Charles VII. in favour of one John Stuart, who had served under him. The Marquis de Ruvigny wrote to Louis XIV. on October 20th, 1667 : " The Duchess of Richmond, formerly Miss Stuart, is preparing to go to France soon, to request your Majesty to place her husband in possession of the estate of Aubigny. There are some here who believe that it is her purpose to attach herself to the Queen-Mother of England and take the place of the late Countess of Guildford. She despairs of a reconciliation, and she is right."[2]

[1] Charles to Madame. August 26th, 1667. [2] C. A. 91.

That some such project was seriously contemplated is evident from a letter addressed to the Duchess by Henry Coventry, one of the envoys at Breda, who had been requested by her to persuade the French ambassadors in Holland to broach the matter of Aubigny to Louis XIV. on their return to France.

Breda, August 5th, st. n. 1667.

Madam

I received the honoure of a Letter from Your Grace of the 12th of July, and though I should be loth to be thought guilty of so moderate a zeal to your service, as that anything could increase my diligence or resolution in promoting that, yet I must acknowledge, I should be much more criminal, should I make the least omission after having received orders under your hand.

Your Letter came somewhat late, yet opportunely enough, Monsr. L'Estrade and Monsr. Courtin being that day at Dinir with me. My Lord Holles and my self pressed them (with) all the earnestness we could in the King's, His Highness Royal's, and (what possibly had no less force than them) your own Name, and they have promised to endeavour with all the interest they have, that My Lord Duke, and Your Grace, may have the satisfaction you desire concerning D'Aubigny.

That I past not by Cobham in my last journey

to and from London, was not that I had forgott who lived there, or the Duty I owed ; but I was so impatient of seeing you delivered from the Apprehensions of a Dutch visit, that I chose rather to forfeit the happiness of seeing your Grace, than by that delay to contribute an hour to your disquiett, which I hope will now be at an end, a Peace being signed, and Sir John Coventry gone with it to bring the Ratification : that done I hope we shall have leave to return, and I to wait on my Lord Duke and Your Grace at Cobham, and to beg his performance of his promise of a Lodge where you shall see me of an insignificant Ambassador become one of the trustiest keepers in Kent, which is now one of the best parts of Christendome since you are there. Madam, I pray pardon this importunity, and do me the justice to believe, that as no man hath a juster and therefore greater esteem of your Perfections than myself, so none is more unreservedly at your disposal than

   Your Grace's
     most humble and most obedient
       servant, H. C.

My most humble service to my Lord Duke, if he be returned to Cobham.[1]

It is clear, however, that the Duchess regarded a

---

[1] Original letter in the collection of the Marquess of Bath, K.G. at Longleat.

retreat to France as a last resort; she did not intend to exile herself from England so long as there were any chance of her returning to Court and taking up the position to which her rank entitled her. Such a chance seemed for the moment somewhat remote, since Frances was prepared to return to Court only on conditions that would be acceptable to her, whereas the King it was who had the whip-hand, and could impose any conditions he desired upon her return. But when one is young, gay, beautiful, and a Duchess, one is not too prone to regard such difficulties as insuperable. Frances refused to be defeated without a struggle. Her first step was to rally her old friends and admirers round her. Accordingly the end of the year found her installed with her husband in Somerset House, where, having, as it were, raised her standard, she began to hold receptions as she had used to do before her marriage. Even if the King himself would not see her, he was not so ill-natured as to forbid others to do so, and a multitude of courtiers, who had missed her sadly during her retirement, flocked eagerly round her once again, and visited her in the evenings, "for her beauty's sake."[1]

So long as she had been at a safe distance it had been easy for Charles to reiterate his fixed determination never to forgive her; but people began to

---

[1] Pepys. December, 26th, 1667.

wonder whether he would be strong enough to persist now when she was so near to him and the whole Court was ringing once again with praises of her charm and beauty.

The possibility of a reconciliation became the favourite subject of discussion. Everyone had their own version of the facts. Some were sure that the King had owned to a desire to see her, and had even made unsuccessful attempts to persuade her to come to Court again ; others resolutely maintained that in spite of her advances the King was steadfast in his refusal to forgive her. Others again held that, though both Frances and the King were only too eager to make up their quarrel, they were foiled in their intentions by the Duke's jealousy.[1] Some rumour of a reconciliation must have reached the Duchess of Orleans, as she evidently alluded to it in a letter to Charles, which is unfortunately lost. In his reply he wrote : " You were misinformed in your intelligence concerning the Duchess of Richmond ; if you were as well acquainted with a little fantastical gentleman call'd Cupide as I am, you would neither wonder nor take ill any suden changes which do happen in the affaires of his conducting, but in this matter there is nothing done in it."[2]

This is sufficiently enigmatical, but it certainly

---

[1] Pepys. December 27th, 1667.
[2] Charles II. to Madame. January 23rd, 1668.

looks as if the "little fantastical gentleman" was beginning to make insidious attempts to undermine His Majesty's resistance. Such at least was the common talk. Even Ruvigny changed his mind, and wrote to Lionne[1] in February saying that a reconciliation was imminent. Lady Castlemaine too became apprehensive, and retired to bed "ill more in mind than in body." In Ruvigny's opinion the gift of Berkshire House, which the King now made to her, was a hint that her presence at Whitehall would no longer be congenial to him.

Although everyone knew that the King had by now made up his mind to give in, yet, from some scruples of pride maybe, he still hesitated to take the final step. Weeks passed by, and he still hung back. Then something happened that banished his pride and roused his natural generosity. The Duchess of Richmond fell seriously ill with the small-pox Charles at once caused her to be told that all was forgiven, and that he no longer harboured any resentment against her. As soon as it was possible for him to see her he hastened to her side and constantly visited her during her convalescence. She was never in danger of her life, but it was greatly feared that the beauty which had won all hearts would be destroyed by the malignant disease. Few believed that she would ever be the same again.

[1] C.A. 91. February 20th, 1668.

"The yonge Dutchis of Richman hathe the small pox and is very full, soe that all beleave her bewty will be spoyled which is a sad business."[1] Pepys was even more pessimistic. "All do conclude she will be wholly spoiled, which is the greatest instance of the uncertainty of beauty that could be in this age; but then," he proceeds consolingly, "she hath had the benefit of it to be first married, and to have kept it so long, under the greatest temptations of a King, and yet without the least imputation."[2] The worthy diarist had conveniently forgotten the imputations he himself had been wont to cast upon her before Evelyn had convinced him of her virtue; but it is at least gratifying to know that he still held the more favourable opinion of her morals. Charles himself was most concerned about the effect the disease would have on Frances's looks. "I cannot tell whether the Duchesse of Richmond will be much marked with the small-pox, she has many and I fear they will at least do her no good." So he wrote to his sister on April the 4th, 1668, adding somewhat caustically: "For her husband, he cannot alter from what he is, lett her be never so much changed."

With his mind full of the sinister rumours abroad as to the ravages the disease had wrought upon her, Pepys was particularly distressed at the sight of a

[1] M. Elmes to Sir Ralph Verney, March 26th, 1668. Original letter in the collection of Sir Harry Verney, Bart., at Claydon House.
[2] Pepys. March 26th, 1668.

portrait of her completed by the painter Cooper just before her illness. " It would make a man weep," he cries, " to see what she was then and what she is like to be, by people's discourse now."[1] Fortunately such reports were to prove much exaggerated, though one of Frances's wonderful eyes was somewhat affected.[2] Her loss of beauty thereby cannot have been very considerable, for at any rate it did not lessen her charm in the eyes of the King, who became so enthralled in her presence that he actually forgot to write to his dearest Minette. " I have so often asked your pardon for omitting writing to you as I am almost ashamed to do it now ; the truth is the last weeke I absolutely forgott it till it was too late, for I was at the Duchesse of Richmond's, who, you know, I have not seene this twelve months ; and shee put it out of my heade that it was post day. She is not much marked with the small pox, and I must confesse this last affliction made me pardon all that is past, and I cannot hinder myselfe from wishing her very well, and I hope shee will not be much changed, as soon as her eye is well, for she has a very great defluction in it and even some danger of haveing a blemish in it, but now, I beleeve, the worst is past."[3]

[1] Pepys. March 30th, 1668.
[2] Ruvigny to Louis XIV. May 21st, 1668. C.A. 91. In the ducal chemist's bill about this time are many entries for ' cataplasmes for the eyes and eye water.' B.M. Add MSS. 21,950.
[3] Charles to Madame. May 7th, 1668.

La Belle Stuart 155

There was general apprehension lest the return of Frances to Court should lead to trouble between those who favoured her and those who supported Lady Castlemaine, for the Court seemed disposed to take sides.[1] But for some reason or other Lady Castlemaine, though she was scarcely disposed to welcome Frances with open arms, did not seem to resent her reappearance. She was no less weary of the King as a lover than he was of her, since her own tastes in that particular were as catholic as his, and she was perfectly willing to do without him in that capacity so long as he remained openly on friendly terms with her, and, more important still, continued to satisfy her material needs. She now took up her residence at Berkshire House, and occupied herself in furnishing and amorous intrigues. The King did not fail to visit her frequently, but, as Ruvigny told Louis XIV., she was no more now to him than a good friend.[2]

Frances did not move to Whitehall at once. For the present she remained at Somerset House, where Charles often came to visit her. Once, indeed, his visit was paid in so unconventional a fashion as to cause a scandal.[3] One Sunday evening when the King had already ordered his coach to take him into the park with the guards in attendance, he suddenly

[1] Pepys. May 8th, 1668.   [2] CA. 91. May 21st, 1668.
[3] Pepys. May 19th, 1668.

changed his mind and determined to pay the Duchess of Richmond a visit. It would be pleasant to go by water on this early summer evening, so His Majesty alone, or, as some say, with one attendant, leapt into a rowing-boat and sculled down the river to Somerset House. But it was growing late, and when he landed he found that the garden-door had been closed for the night. In Charles's place no doubt a great many kings would have retired and sought some more dignified mode of entry than did His Majesty, but then Charles was no ordinary king, and to climb over a garden-wall was a mere trifle after some of the adventures he had experienced during the perilous times before his Restoration. So the King clambered over the wall, and gave London something to talk about.

Many weighty conclusions have been drawn from this boyish escapade of the King's. Some have discerned in it a clandestine assignation affording irrefutable proof that the Duchess of Richmond had now become his mistress. But, if this be true, was ever intrigue more clumsily and carelessly conducted? If the King's visit was pre-arranged, what could have been his purpose in ordering his coach and guards and then deliberately drawing attention to his movements by leaving them to wait in the Courtyard at Whitehall, while he betook himself off elsewhere? And if Frances was apprised of his coming, surely he and she between them possessed influence enough to have the garden-door kept open? Of course it is always possible that a jealous husband, getting wind of what was toward, spent the evening with the key in his pocket! It is difficult to see why it should have been considered unlikely that Charles II., than whom no more thoroughly human person ever sat upon a throne, should have simply indulged the caprice of the moment, and enjoyed one of those fantastic adventures which appealed so much to his peculiar sense of humour.

The King and Queen were now on the very best of terms. Charles had lately formed the estimable habit of supping with his wife every evening. Her recent miscarriage had once more aroused all his tenderness for her, and he did his best to console her in their disappointment. Curiously enough the hope of an heir was perhaps stronger now than it had ever been, for, as Charles wrote to his sister: "I am glad that 'tis evident she was with childe, which I will not deny to you till now I did feare she was not capable of. The phesisians do intend to put her into a course phesique which they are confident will make her holde faster next time."[1]

Catherine was delighted to see Frances again, and they speedily renewed their old friendship. At a grand supper which the Duchess of Richmond gave to their Majesties it was announced that the Queen

[1] Charles to Madame. May 7th, 1668.

had been pleased to appoint her one of her Ladies of the Bed-chamber.[1] This appointment carried with it lodgings at Whitehall, and a few weeks later the Duke and Duchess of Richmond moved into their new house in the Bowling Green,[2] a delightful pavilion overlooking the river on the one side and the Garden of Statues on the other.

Now that Frances had resumed her place in the constellation of beauties at Whitehall, Pepys was able to resume the pleasurable diversion of commenting upon her appearance. "Alone to the Park," he records on August the 18th, 1668, " but there were few coaches: among the few there were our two great beauties, my lady Castlemaine and Richmond: the first time I saw the latter since she had the smallpox. I had much pleasure to see them, but I thought they were strange to one another." Such a circumstance should scarcely have astonished Pepys ! He had not yet seen the Duchess close to since her illness, but he was to be vouchsafed a glimpse on August the 30th. " So I to the Park, and there walk an hour or two ; and in the King's garden, and saw the Queen and ladies walk ; and I did steal some apples off the trees ; and here did see my Lady Richmond who is of a noble person as ever

---

[1] Ruvigny to Lionne. June 28th, 1668. C.A. 91.
[2] Cal. Stat. Pap. Dom. 1668. August 5th. These were possibly the same lodgings as the Duke had occupied before his marriage to Frances.

I did see, but her face worse than it was considerably by the smallpox, her sister is also very handsome." The sister was Sophia, who had come over with the Queen-Mother as one of her dressers in 1663. She married Henry Bulkely, fourth son of Thomas, 1st Viscount Bulkely, and Master of the Household to Charles II.

Even if Frances's face had become considerably worse than it was, it must still have held an irresistible attraction for Pepys, since on September the 9th 1668 comes the following entry in his Diary : " To the Duke of Richmond's lodgings by his desire, by letter, yesterday. I find him at his lodgings in the little building in the bowling-green, at White Hall, that was begun to be built by Captain Rolt. They are fine rooms. I did hope to see his lady ; but she, I hear, is in the country. His business was about his yacht, and he seems a mighty good-natured man, and did presently write me a warrant for a doe from Cobham, when the season comes, buck season being past. I shall make much of this acquaintance, that I may live to see his lady near !"

CHAPTER VII

Scandalous rumours—The Duchess's affection for her husband—Lord Mulgrave's 'Elegy'—The Court at Newmarket—Louis XIV. sends over the Abbé Pregnani—His ill-success—The state of the Duke of Richmond's finances—His journey to France—Frances looks after his affairs—Lord Bath's letter—Frances quarrels with Jermyn—Ashley's schemes for the Duke—They come to nothing—Louis XIV proposes to send Madame to England—The difficulties in the way overcome—Madame at Dover—Louise de Keroualle—Death of Madame—Frances at Cobham—Hunting in Charles II's. days—Letter from Frances to the Duke—Frances in attendance on the Queen—Their escapade at Audley End—A masked ball—The Queen's ballet—The Court in Norfolk—Charles II's. alleged indiscretion at Raynham—The King at Euston—Mock-marriage with Louise de Keroualle—Richmond appointed ambassador to Denmark—Rumours as to the reasons—Why they should be discounted—Rivalry of Frances and Louise de Keroualle.

When that part of the world which is prone to think the worst of its fellow-men—and it is no inconsiderable part—has made up its mind to think ill of anyone, nothing will divert it from its preconceived ideas. Those who had disbelieved Frances Stuart's professions of virtue were not going to be turned from their uncharitable opinion of her by the circumstances of her marriage, as she had hoped they would be. The scandal about her, far from being silenced, was actually increased. Many even, who believed that she had remained chaste up to the time of her marriage, now declared that she had consented to grant the King her favours when she returned to Court as Duchess of Richmond, and could no longer claim to be a shy maiden afraid of love. This assumption was naturally based partly on the reconciliation between Charles and Frances and the obvious predilection he displayed for her society, but partly also on the general opinion that she could not possibly be in love with her husband. Whence this idea arose it is impossible to say, but it may well be imagined that it was fostered and encouraged by all those who were anxious for purposes of their own to see the friendship between the King and the Duchess develop into a more intimate but less honourable connection. But whatever may have been the reasons which led their contemporaries to think that there was no love lost between the Duke and Duchess of Richmond, posterity has been afforded better evidence for judging of the state of their feelings. Their correspondence reveals a mutual trust and an unremitting devotion to each other's interests, and shows that there was always a very real and deep affection between them. At the time, however, there were few who did not imagine that the Duchess's married life was a continued misery, and that her husband was both cruel and unfaithful to her. She was pitied by everyone but herself. In the light of the relations that are now known to have subsisted between Frances and her husband it is amusing to read the extravagant elegy written to her by Lord Mulgrave, a most ardent admirer, whose portrayal of the Duke's character was in all likelihood not a little influenced by an obvious desire to take his place. The poem must indeed have filled Frances with puzzled amusement, if he ever had the impertinence to show it to her.

[1] *Elegy to the Duchess of R......*

Thou lovely slave to a rude husband's will,
By nature us'd so well, by him so ill !
For all that grief we see your mind endure,
Your glass presents you with a pleasing cure ;
Those maids you envy for their happier state,
To have your form, would gladly have your fate ;
And of like slavery each wife complains,
Without such beauty's help to bear her chains.
Husbands like him we every where may see,
But where can we behold a wife like thee ?
While to a tyrant you by fate are ty'd,
By love you tyrannize o'er all beside :
Those eyes, tho' weeping, can no pity move ;
Worthy our grief ! More worthy of our love !
You while so fair (do Fortune what she please)
Can be no more in pain, than we at ease :
Unless unsatisfied with all our vows,
Your vain ambition so unbounded grows,

[1] Works of John Sheffield, Earl of Mulgrave, Marquis of Normanby, and Duke of Buckingham.

That you repine a husband should escape
Th' united force of such a face and shape.
If so, alas, for all those charming pow'rs
Your case is just as desperate as ours.
Expect that birds should only sing to you,
And, as you walk, that every tree should bow;
Expect those statues as you pass should burn;
And that with wonder men should statues turn;
Such beauty is enough to give things life,
But not to make a husband love his wife:
A husband, worse than statues, or than trees;
Colder than those, less sensible than these.
Then from so dull a care your thoughts remove,
And waste not sighs you only owe to Love.
'Tis pity, sighs from such a breast should part,
Unless to ease some doubtful lover's heart;
Who dies because he must too justly prize
What yet the dull Possessor does despise.
Thus, precious jewels among Indians grow
Who, nor their use, nor wondrous value know;
But we for those bright treasures tempt the Main,
And hazard life for what the fools disdain.

The author of this impassioned address was a young man of the same age as Frances herself. As yet he had shown no signs of the interest in political matters which was to absorb him later on in life; he was known chiefly as a fervent devotee of the Muses and an intimate friend of the poet Dryden, though, like most young noblemen of his day, he had not neglected military pursuits and had served with great gallantry during the Dutch wars as a volunteer on board the fleet, under Prince Rupert and the Duke of Albemarle.

In the spring of this year (1669) the Court went to Newmarket, where the chief diversion then as in these present days was horse-racing. Now that there was peace once more between England and France, Louis XIV. resumed his attempts to gain complete control over Charles II's. foreign policy. His first special envoy, an ambassador, as it were, to the King in his personal capacity, was an Italian charlatan, the Abbé Pregnani, who cast horoscopes and pretended to foretell the future. If it had been hoped to play upon Charles II's. superstition, no more unfortunate an occasion could have been devised for the endeavour. The Abbé was far from being at home in the sporting atmosphere of the English Court ; he was bewildered by what seemed to him the childish amusements of this outlandish people, and the constant exercise he was forced to take reduced him to a condition of extreme fatigue. Nor was he more fortunate in that less energetic pursuit wherein his prophetic gifts might have been expected to help him. Here he failed utterly, as appears from a letter from Charles II. to Madame (March the 22nd, 1669) " L'Abbé Pregnani was here most part of the time, and I beleeve will give you some account of it, but not that he lost his mony upon confidence that the starrs could tell which horse would winn, for he

La Belle Stuart 165

had the ill luck to foretell three times wrong together, and James[1] beleeved him, so much as he lost his mony upon the same score." With his characteristic good humour he wrote to his sister a few days later begging her not to allow this failure on the part of the Abbé to destroy her faith in him, since he was apparently merely testing a new system!

The Duke of Richmond had not improved his financial position by his marriage, and he was beginning to wonder whither to turn for money. For some time past the Earl of St. Alban's and other friends, both English and French, had been endeavouring on his behalf to persuade Louis XIV. to put him in possession of the fief of Aubigny, of which he was hereditary duke; and now he heard that his wish would be granted, if he would go over to France to take formal possession. The Duke set forth immediately, as no possible source of revenue could be neglected. He had recently applied to Charles II. for a 'pension' of £1000 a year, which he considered that his family merited, since it had been ruined by its adherence to the Royalist cause during the years of the Civil War and the Commonwealth. Lord Arlington, who, since the fall of Clarendon, had become the King's chief adviser, promised to do his best to procure it for him.[2] But the Duke knew well that the ways of officialdom are exceedingly slow,

[1] The Duke of Monmouth. [2] Add MSS. 21,947 f.231. 234.

and entrusted to his wife the task of keeping the matter to the fore during his absence. Frances threw herself into the affair with rather too much energy according to Lord Bath,[1] who wrote to the Duke telling him that Lord Arlington hoped soon to bring the matter of the pension to a successful issue. " Of it you shall forthwith have an account from mee, and if not you will be sure to have it from my Lady Dutchesse who is growne soe good a solicitor in your affayres that to speak plainely it is troublesome to herselfe as well as to her frends, and, I feere, prejudiciall to her health, giving her the spleene too often because her frequent solicitations have as yet produced noe effects, which she sayes she would never have more appeared in if not for your sake more than her owne and in obedience to your commands. And for these reasons I have been affrayd sometimes of seeing her Grace in a fortnight, not being able to give her such an account as I would and as shee expects from mee every minute I have the honour to see her, soe that I feare in your absence and service I may run the hazard of loosing my Ladyes good opinion, which I hope at your retourne you will endeavour to restore to mee as a jewell of too great valew to be lost, and not let me suffer when I am in noe fault, nor for the slowe paths which statesmen usually walke in."[2]

[1] John Granville or Grenville, Earl of Bath, son of the famous West-Country soldier, Sir Bevil Grenville.
[2] Add MSS. 21,947 f. 235.

It was quite true that the Duchess of Richmond's nerves had been seriously affected by her unceasing efforts to serve her husband's interest, for this summer there occurred one of the very few occasions on which she was so far shaken from her accustomed equability as to indulge in a violent quarrel.

The Queen was once more expecting a child, and the prospect caused some bad feeling between the partizans of the King and those of the Duke of York, whose children would naturally be cut off from the direct line of succession by the birth of an heir to the Crown. The suppressed resentments burst into flame at a party given by Lord Bath. The host raised his glass to the future child and asked the whole company to drink its health. But the Duchess of Richmond, who was always rather aggressively devoted to the Queen, noting that among those present was the younger Jermyn, one of the Duke's most active supporters, with more loyalty than tact proceeded to emphasize the meaning of the toast by requesting him to drink to " The Prince of Wales." Jermyn became nettled and suggested that the Duchess in turn should toast the Prince of Tuscany,[1] an illustrious foreigner, who during his recent visit to England had paid her marked attentions, which scandalous tongues had not failed to comment upon. He knew well enough that nothing could rile Frances

---

[1] Afterwards the Grand Duke Cosmo III.

more than the least insinuation against her virtue. She at once lost her temper, and high words passed between them. Frances afterwards went to the Queen and told her that Jermyn had been unwilling to drink the health of her child. She also complained to the King, but he with his usual good sense refused to take any notice of the affair, and told her plainly that he resented these continual efforts to stir up trouble between his brother and himself.[1]

But though Frances was ready to wear herself out badgering statesmen and worrying her friends to death with her importunities, she would not herself approach the King on the subject. If the pension were granted, it should be as of right for the services of her husband's family, and not as a compliment to herself. Moreover, at the moment she would not have cared to ask a favour of the King, since she was vexed at his refusal to reprimand Jermyn for insulting her. Lord Bristol told the Duke that he could scarcely hope to gain his wishes, while the Duchess failed to respond to His Majesty's attentions with even ' so much as that complaisance which shee owes him in all considerations, nor have I hopes of her minding unless you interpose a greater power than the advice of all her other best friends.'[2]

Meanwhile Lord Ashley,[3] one of the Duke's best

[1] C.A. 94. Colbert de Croissy to Lionnel. May 21, 1669.
[2] Add MSS. 21,947 f. 239.
[3] Afterwards the 1st Earl of Shaftesbury.

friends, came forward with another suggestion for overcoming his financial difficulties. He knew that Richmond had always had diplomatic ambitions and had formerly requested the King to send him on an embassy to the Princes of Italy, so, now that there was a likelihood of an extraordinary embassy being sent to Poland on the election of a new King, he advised him to apply for that post, which would certainly be well paid. Lord Bath also urged him to adopt Ashley's advice. Arlington was approached and found to view the plan with approval. All that remained was to make the application. Ashley's suggestions as to how this should be done are most illuminating. The letter to Lord Arlington, applying for the post, should, he said, be short, ' only mentioning your former desire to him concerning Italy, but that you incline more to this, your ayme being only to render your self usefull and serviceable to His Majesty in whatever he shall think you capable of. I presume to dictate thus much to your grace, because the letter must be shewed the King, and I fear the resentments your grace may have of your ill treatments of late might make you mingle something not soe advantagious. If your Grace approves of this designe pray thinke not of comming over but leave the conduct of this affair to my lord Bath and me; for your absence whatever happens will preserve you from the reflection of a personall refusall; besides, the compassion of a prince of the

Royall family, absent, layd by, and neglected works something, and far more than your presence, being yet in noe greater favor. When the King has by degrees imployed and obliged you I doubt not but he will returne to his kindnes and the reason he has both to trust and favor you before other men.'[1]

Ashley was obviously anxious to do the Duke a good turn, but he knew that the King had always disliked and despised him, and that he had never forgiven him for marrying Frances. To obtain any favour for him would be difficult enough in any circumstances, but it would be impossible, if the Duke himself appeared in the affair, since he was liable to be rather too outspoken on the subject of his grievances. Decidedly he would be better out of the way for the time being. Luckily Richmond himself had the sense to appreciate this, and consented to remain in France. Moreover, he framed his letter of application to Arlington on the principles Ashley had laid down.[2] To Frances he wrote that he would not be returning to England as soon as he had expected, and that either Lord Ashley or Lord Bath would explain his reasons to her. The negotiation was being kept secret, and he conceivably did not care to say too much in a letter that might be opened. The ordinary post in these days appears to have been most unreliable.

[1] Add MSS. 21,947 ff. 245,247.
[2] Add MSS. 21,947 f. 248 (copy of his letter).

Frances had not yet had an opportunity of learning the reason for his continued absence before she next wrote to her husband.

To the Duke of Richmond and Lenox at the Queene Mother of inglands Court att Paris or Collombe

My Deare Lord,   Aug ye . . .

I reseved yours this day in which you writ me word you shall not returne soe soon as you intended the reason of which you say my (Lord) Ashley or Lord of Bathe will tell me. I have seene neyther since I reseved yours and would not faile writting by this post. My (Lord) Ashley is out of Towne ; but my Lord of Bathe I will endever to speake with soe soone as I can, and give him your Letter. By the last post I sent you A Bill of Exchange for 400 pound ; I hope it came safe to your hands and that by the next I shall have it confirmed by you ; which pray doe not neglect as soon as is possible, becasse if that should miscary I have an other to find you, and I feare very much that our Letters are lost becase I did not heere from you by neythere of the 2 posts before the last ; and I am confident tis not your falght but rather my misfortune or Ellse peoples curiosity ; for many of yours appeere to me to have bine opened. On monday next the King begins his Jurny towards the west ; how long he will stay is not certaine. I will not troble

you now any farther; but to desire you will
beleeve me as truly I am
>Your most affectionat wife
>>and servant
>>>F. Richmond and Lenox.

Last night poor littele blake Dike[1] dyed but noe body can tell of what, and all the world could not make him take any kind of thinge after he first sikened which was not 2 dayes before he dyed.
The widdow presents her humble servis to you. My duty pray to my Mother and desire her to excuse my not writing this post for my head akes so extreemly I know not what I doe.[2]

But though Arlington really tried his best, the King refused to grant the Duke's request for the embassy. Richmond was deeply offended. He was convinced that the King's refusal was due to personal dislike, as it well may have been, though the reasons given, even if not the true ones, were sound enough and certainly threw no discredit on the Duke. His Majesty had told Lord Arlington that he did not think fit to send any embassy to Poland for the

---

[1] In what capacity Black Dick served the Duke is uncertain, but there is an entry in one of the bills of the ducal household: "March 14 1667. To Black-Dick for a weekes Board-wages and a shooe for his horse, and for his passage downe by water to Cobham. 8s. 6d." Add MSS. 21,950 f. 63.

[2] Add MSS. 21,957 f. 253.

present, and that if he did, it would certainly not be proper to send an envoy of the rank of the Duke of Richmond.[1] At any rate Charles II's. resentment at the Duke's marriage must have died down by now ; for he was no longer in love with the Duchess. Colbert de Croissy even goes so far as to say that he had actually repelled advances on her part. According to him she had been intriguing during this summer with the object of regaining the King's affections, but without success now that his roving fancy had for the moment settled on Nell Gwynne.[2] It is more likely that what the French Ambassador took for attempts to win the King's love were in reality attempts to obtain his money. After Lord Bristol's hint the Duke had assuredly written to his Duchess informing her that their financial embarrassments made it imperative that she should be more civil to His Majesty.

In November the Duke made another attempt to obtain some employment. The grave illness of the Lord Chamberlain, the Earl of Manchester, had given rise to the impression that his high office would soon be vacant. The Duke of Richmond was one of the most eager aspirants, and left no stone unturned in his efforts to obtain his desires. In case he should be chosen, he offered to relinquish all his

[1] Add MSS. 21,947 f. 264.
[2] C.A. 95 Colbert to Lionne. Nov. 17th, 1669.

other appointments and any claim he might have on the King's favour. He not only himself wrote to this effect to Lord Arlington, but also persuaded Ralph Montagu, the English Ambassador in Paris, to write urging his claims. In addition he authorized Montagu to tell Arlington that he could count on the Duke of Richmond's support against the Duke of Buckingham, with whom he had recently quarrelled, and who was now endeavouring to compass his downfall. The Duchess of Orleans also wrote to her brother soliciting the place for the Duke of Richmond; but this she did less for his own sake than for that of Frances, to whom she had always remained a devoted friend. These endeavours did not, however, proceed further than the initial stages, since Manchester's illness did not prove fatal and there was therefore no longer any immediate prospect of the office falling vacant.[1]

Louis XIV. now considered that the time had come to send over an envoy of a different stamp from Pregnani, if he were ever to obtain that complete control over Charles II's. foreign policy, which he so ardently desired. The best agent he could have would be the Duchess of Orleans, who had already become the intermediary between the two kings in all their most secret negotiations. Although her affection for her brother was very deep, her up-

[1] Add MSS. 21,948 f. 133. Hist. MSS. Comm. Report. Buccleuch MSS. 437 and 450.

"MADAME"

[face p. 174

bringing had made her sympathies more French than English, and she could be relied upon not to betray the country of her adoption. Moreover, she was probably as fond of Louis as she was of Charles, for the brief love-affair that had taken place between them on her first arrival at the French Court after her marriage had left them with a very real affection for each other. Who could be found more suited to go to England and negotiate a treaty of alliance ? Charles was longing to see his favourite sister again, and would be overjoyed if she came. The only obstacles were the suspicion of the Dutch and the jealousy of Monsieur, the Duke of Orleans, who proved to the full that it is possible for a husband to be madly jealous of his wife without any love for her. An opportunity of evading the first of these obstacles occurred in the spring of 1670, when Louis decided to visit Flanders with his Court to view the province lately ceded to France by Spain What could be more natural than that Henriette of Orleans should take advantage of her proximity to the shores of England to cross over and visit the brother whom she had not seen for so long ? Even the congenitally suspicious Dutchmen could scarcely attach any political significance to so natural an action. But Monsieur was more difficult, and obstinately refused to allow her to go, though he intimated that he might consider the question, if it were arranged that he should accompany her. But this would not have suited Henriette and Louis. Monsieur had not been made privy to the secret negotiations between the two kings, and his wife was afraid that his presence would jeopardize the success of her mission. Monsieur thereupon relapsed into his former position of unqualified refusal. But too much depended on this visit for Louis, who was in general meticulously observant of his brother's rights, to allow them to interfere with his cherished schemes. It was plainly intimated to Monsieur that he must yield, which he did with a bad grace, stipulating that Henriette was not to go further than Dover, certainly not to London, and that her stay was not to exceed three days. This he did because he knew that Charles was anxious that his sister should not remain at Dover, owing to the poorness of the accommodation there and the inconvenience of bringing the Queen and the Duchess of York there too. Louis XIV. and Henriette consented to Monsieur's conditions, knowing full well that, when once Henriette was across the Channel, it would be found possible to modify these arrangements.

Charles II. was delighted at her coming and prepared to give her a right royal reception. At first it seems to have been intended that the Queen should go over to Calais to meet her, attended by the Duchess of Richmond, Lady Castlemaine, Lady Marshal, and Lady Gerard, but this idea was abandoned. Instead she was met at sea by Charles himself with the

Duke of York, Prince Rupert, and the Duke of Monmouth. The Queen and her ladies afterwards met her on land. The Duchess of Richmond had travelled down to Dover in some state in a coach drawn by six horses, the bill for which was still not fully paid off at the time of her husband's death.[1]

After all the Duchess of Orleans stayed in Dover for nearly a fortnight and succeeded in negotiating the treaties, which bound England to aid in the destruction of Holland, arranged for the ultimate conversion of the whole country to Roman Catholicism, and made Charles II. virtually the pensioner of France. In the intervals of the negotiations all manner of festivities were arranged, and it was at these that one of Madame's Maids of Honour, Louise de Keroualle, first attracted Charles II's. attention. This was the lady who as Duchess of Portsmouth was to be the royal mistress in the succeeding years of the reign. Although Charles II. instantly fell a victim to her charms, Madame firmly refused his request that she should be left behind in England. Louis XIV. was less delicate about acting as a pander, especially when he would benefit politically, and with his connivance she returned to England a year later, henceforth to assume the part of secret agent between the two kings in place of Madame, who died suddenly a few days after her return to France, her death being at that time attributed, with injustice

---

[1] Egerton MSS. 2435. f. 23.

as it seems, to the malignity of her husband, who was popularly supposed to have poisoned her in a glass of chicory-water.

After leaving Dover Frances proceeded to Cobham Hall, where she was joined by her mother. The Duke had gone to Scotland on affairs connected with his rights as Lord High Admiral in that kingdom. Frances often wrote to tell him how she was endeavouring to console herself during his absence.

Cobham the 31st of August.

My Deare Lord

By my not heereing from you this last weeke I conclude you have begune your Jurney into the west, but by that time this can arrive to Endenburg I susspose you will be returned theyther; till today wee have had very fine weather and I hope shall have more good of the same, for I take great pleasure in hunting; meethinkes your park is finer this yeere then ever I saw it and the new stand you built since my comeing from Dover is very fine, I was in it the other day myselfe but could not perswad my Mother go up for all the world. I can send you no newes but that I heere the Court is to return to London on the 5th of September; by my next you shall know the certainty of it, but now pray be content with the assureance of my beeing very faitfully your affectionate wife and servant

F. Richmond and Lenox.

Our friend Mr. Titus has sould his government of Deal to my Lord of Bristol for his son. I heere my Lord of Essex is in holland and dayly expected heere, but I am sure he is not yet com for I make every body that goes to graves-end inquier if he hath pased that way.

Mr Sidley and Mr. Fane have bine heere this 3 dayes and all the naybors heere about have very kindly bine to see me, I only want fair weather to return them thankes.[1]

The hunting which gave such pleasure to the Duchess was in those days a somewhat peculiar diversion. The deer were driven up to a stand, whence the sportsmen of the period would take pot-shots at them. Possibly, however, the comparatively primitive nature of their fire-arms introduced a greater element ot chance into the sport than would be expected under modern conditions. Perhaps too the stability of the 'stands' was precarious, since Mrs Stuart seemed so reluctant to risk her neck in mounting one.

When the Court at last returned to London, the high office which Frances held made it necessary for her to leave the country and resume her duties near the Queen. She was at Whitehall when she received a letter from her husband asking her if she had heard

[1] Add MSS. 21,947 f. 257.

anything of some rumour to his discredit which appeared to have got abroad. She replied :

" My deare Lord

The Queen's comeing to London yesterday caused me to do so too, haveing bine informed shee was not pleased with me for not waiting on her at Hamton Court. At my return I reseved a letter of yours in which you desire an account of your building at Cobham. Truly I cannot give you any, for except sleeping time, I was very littel in the house. But I would have informed myselfe better if I had known you desired it. All I can assure you is that you have a carefull and trusty person there of Mr. Mapelsden, for by what I do see I judg of that I do not. I am very sorry you were not well when you writ last, though by this time I hope you are ; at least I wish with all my hart it were in my power to do you any good or servis whereby you might see how faithfully I am yours. As for the account you desire of me conserning that scandellous report you say is maid of you, I am certenly the person (in all Ingland) that can give you the most imperfect one, for thinges of that nature people are not used to entertaine the party conserned with all, (thayer too displeasing). That littel I did heere of it, as I told you in my last, I could not possible beleeve, but looked upon it as a mallisous thinge raysed by some of your enemyes, though I beleeve it is past the industry of man to find out who were furst the authers of it ; for you say they are some of the Court, and oft I know it may be soe. All I can say is that what ever may be talked of it out of my heereing I knowe not, but I protest I heard much more of it in the Countrey, that being a place where there is much less to discourse of as well as less veryetty of subjects, and where people are better bred thay take more care of not discovering those thinges which they know cannot but render thayer company very disagreeable. Last night when I came to Towne I heard an other false report that trobled me much, which was the death of my Lord Ashly; but sending today to inquier of him I heere he has bine ill but is now much better. My Lord of Essex and my Lady are this day expected in Town as I am informed by theyer servants (for I was to have waited on my lady, but she has bine ever since her comeing into England, which has not bine above 3 or fower days, att Chaabury[1] to see my Lady Bettey. The King is so much pleased with Windsor that he intends to be theyer all the next summer, and his great offissers are goeing to build theyer. About the 20th of this month he intends a juerny of ten or twelve dayes to Newmarket. This is all the newes I know haveing bine yet but littel at Court since I came.

[1] Cashiobury, the Earl of Essex's house in Hertfordshire ?

Farewell, my deare Lord, I will not hold you any longer now but to assure you I am and so you shall ever find me

   Your most affectionat
     wife and servant
      F. Richmond and Lennox.

I had forgot to tell you that though you say you reseve but few of mine I never have fayeled writing to you twice a weeke at the least ever since you were in Scotland, most commonly 3 times, which is every post; were it not for feare of trobling you I am sure I should never faile any." [1]

That the Queen should have been offended because Frances had not been to see her at Hampton Court shows that the old friendship between them had been renewed, as does also the story of a ludicrous escapade in which they both took part in the autumn of this year, when the Court was at Audley End, which the King had recently bought from Lord Suffolk. The Queen one day took the fancy into her head of going in disguise to a fair which was being held near by. She chose as her companions the Duchesses of Richmond and Buckingham, and enlisted the services of three gentlemen, one of whom was old Sir Bernard Gascoign, who had fought for Charles I. in the Civil War and had narrowly escaped being hanged by the Roundheads after the fall of Colchester. The

[1] Add MSS. 21,947 f. 259.

La Belle Stuart

second was a Mr. Roper, but the name of the third has not come down to posterity. The Queen and the two Duchesses arrayed themselves in red petticoats and other such garments as they considered appropriate to the parts they had to play, while the men did their best to disguise themselves as country bumpkins. And so they gaily went off to the fair, the ladies riding pillion behind their cavaliers on cart-horses. But they had all so overdone their disguise, and looked so unlike the real country folk that their arrival, instead of passing unremarked as they had hoped, created a sensation. A curious crowd followed them eagerly everywhere they went, and when they stopped at a booth and made some purchases, the Queen choosing a pair of yellow stockings for her sweetheart and Sir Bernard demanding some gloves stitched with blue for his, those about them soon perceived from their language that they were not what they professed to be. Then who in the world were they? This was the question freely asked by the ever-growing crowd about them. As ill fortune would have it there was a woman amongst them, who had once seen the Queen dining in state and had recognized her. The news of the strangers' identity spread like wildfire, and presently the whole fair had flocked about them. Once discovered, there was nothing for it but to take to flight, and the adventurers regained their horses as quickly as they could and started back to Audley End. But they were not the only ones who had come mounted to the fair; such of the crowd as had horses or could find room behind the rider on somebody else's steed deserted the fair and pursued the greater attraction. Nor did they abandon the pursuit till the Court Gate at Audley End was shut in their faces.[1]

The fashion for attending balls and parties masked came in this winter and gave the courtiers much amusement. Colbert de Croissy wrote to Lionne on December the 15th: "The King of England, the Queen, and all their Court were masked last Saturday, at a lawyer's party where they danced a good deal, but truly with the exception of the Queen and several ladies of her suite, all the others and the men too were crowded together in a confusion which gave rise to many little adventures which have made this form of amusement even more to their taste."[2] Mademoiselle de Keroualle was taken to this same party by the Prince of Orange, who had abandoned his habitual reserve with women to worship at her feet. The King also paid marked attentions to her, but she had not yet become his mistress as rumour had stated.[3]

The Queen was now almost continually with the Duchesses of Richmond and Buckingham, preferring

---

[1] Letter from Mr. Henshaw to Sir Robert Paston. Historical MSS. Commission 6th Report. Ingilby Papers p. 367.
[2] C.A. 98.
[3] Ibid.

them to any other ladies at Court, and showing her preference rather markedly. On one occasion when she and her ladies were riding at Hampton Court and Lady Marshal and Lady Gerrard were following in her coach, it came on to rain. The Queen got into her coach and invited her two favourites to come with her, while the other two unfortunate ladies were turned out to find their way home over the common in the rain.[1]

The favour extended to her by the Queen together with her own innate love of amusement made the Duchess of Richmond's post as Lady of the Bedchamber most congenial to her; her presence at Court was constantly demanded, and the succession of balls, masquerades, and ballets gave her the fullest opportunities of displaying her marvellous gift for dress and indulging in her favourite occupation of dancing. In February 1671 she figured with the Duchesses of Buckingham and Monmouth in a magnificent ballet arranged by the Queen. The music was specially composed for the occasion, and most elaborate costumes were devised, there being three changes of costume for each performer during the course of the evening. So high were the expectations aroused by the reports circulated beforehand that there was an abnormal demand for the privilege of watching the performance, and those

[1] Hatton Correspondence I. 64.

who desired to have a good view of it were obliged to arrive at the Palace several hours before the ballet was timed to begin.[1] Frances was also in attendance on the Queen when a royal progress was made to Norfolk in the autumn of 1671. It was during this visit that the King is supposed to have become so drunk one evening at Lord Townshend's at Raynham that he actually boasted to the Duke of Richmond that he had triumphed over his wife's virtue.[2] This is not the sort of revelation usually made by anyone with a pretence to good taste or good manners, and if Charles so far forgot himself on this occasion as to make such a remark at all, whether it were true or false, he must have been very drunk, so drunk indeed that his statement can hardly be taken as a proof of the Duchess's infidelity to her husband. Though truth is liable to out when the wine flows freely, there are times when it flows so fast that truth itself is drowned. Be it agreed then that His Majesty was right royally drunk that evening at Lord Townshend's, for if he was not it were impossible to condone his conversation. At any rate, whatever may have been said, the Duke of Richmond's faith in his wife remained unshaken.

From Raynham the King proceeded to Euston, Lord Arlington's country-seat, where he was met by

[1] Hist. MSS. Comm. Report. Rutland MSS. II. 22. Lady Mary Bertie to Katherine Noel.

[2] Lord Dartmouth, Notes to Burnet's History of His Own Time.

the Queen and her ladies, who had remained at Norwich while he had visited several places in the neighbourhood. It was while the King was staying at Euston that a mock-marriage is reputed to have taken place between him and Louise de Keroualle. Evelyn, who was staying in the house at the time, declared that if such a ceremony took place he himself was certainly not present at it, but his object in making this statement seems to have been more to clear himself from the implication of having committed so heinous a lapse from his lofty standard of propriety than to deny that such an incident actually occurred. He was far from regarding the rumour as unlikely, since he acknowledged that the young lady's behaviour even during the day-time had been wanton in the extreme. 'However,' he concluded with unctuous gravity, "it was with confidence believed she was first made a Miss, as they call these unhappy creatures, with solemnity at this time."[1] The conclusions falsely drawn at the time of the former 'frolick' with Frances were drawn with more justice on this occasion. It soon became common knowledge that the lovely French girl had become the King's mistress.

At the end of this year Charles II. at length consented to fulfil the Duke of Richmond's ambition to be sent on a foreign mission. He was appointed

[1] Evelyn 9th and 10th October, 1671.

Ambassador Extraordinary to Denmark with the task of inducing the Danes to join the Anglo-French alliance against Holland. The King's motives for sending the Duke rather than anyone else were quite consistent with the reasons he had formerly given for refusing to let him go to Poland or Italy. It was in his view so essential that in this instance the embassy should be exceptionally splendid and imposing that he overruled Arlington's objection that the brilliance of the Embassy and the exalted rank of the Ambassador would have the effect of making the Swedes jealous.[1]

Considering that the Duke had for some time been demanding without success to be sent on a mission of this kind, it seems most unlikely that the embassy was merely an expedient devised by the King for getting a jealous husband out of the way. If such had been his intention, surely he would have carried it out earlier rather than now, just when he had taken a new mistress to himself, especially as the Duke had never displayed any reluctance to going, but had on the other hand eagerly solicited just such an appointment. It was however freely rumoured that the Duke had been sent into exile in order to leave the field clear for the King's intrigue with his wife. The popular conception of the reasons for his removal

---

[1] Colbert de Croissy to Louis XIV. December 30th, 1671. C. A. 101.

from England is expressed in the following lines from a contemporary satire on a palmist, Madame le Croy.

> " In comes a Duke from mighty place
> And merit, fall'n into disgrace ;
> She views his hand, and bids him joy,
> Calls him his Excellence Vice-Roy.
> With this high character the buble
> Is well content, and pays her double :
> Nor dreams he's banish't with his fleet
> A slave to Patmos or to Creet.
> As Richmond to the Northern Frost,
> And Clarendon to the Irish coast,
> Blinded with pride, senseless of ruin,
> So fools embrace their own undoing."[1]

Even Colbert de Croissy thought that there was some such reason for sending the Duke away from England. He was convinced that the Duchess was still endeavouring to recapture the King's affections. On the 24th of December 1671 he wrote to Louvois:— " The Duke of Richmond is getting ready to leave as ambassador extraordinary to Denmark, and the King his master has been caressing the Duchess his wife in her husband's presence, at least one can quite well see indications that she is very attractive to the King. Nevertheless Mlle. de Queroel is still in favour and is again taking the King of England to sup and dance at my Lord Arlington's, where I too am invited.

[1] Poems on Affairs of State, Vol. II., 152.

But the Duchess of Richmond is also to be there, and as her greatest talent is dancing, Mlle. de Querouaille may well be defeated by all these parties, and all the more so because she does not know how to conduct herself in her good fortune, having got it into her head that she might yet be Queen of England. She is always talking of the Queen's ailments, which are trifling, as if they were mortal.[1]

It is quite evident that Frances was doing her utmost to defeat Louise de Keroualle, but it does not follow that she wished to supplant her. In the light of her friendship with the Queen it seems incredible that she should have cherished any such idea. Is it not possible that she was actuated not by a desire to gain the King's love for herself but by a determination to prevent anyone else from destroying his love for his wife?

[1] C.A. 101.

CHAPTER VIII

The Duke of Richmond's preparations—He visits the French Ambassador—His arrival in Denmark—His ostentation—Henshaw's position in the embassy—His opinion of the Duke's capacity—Private correspondence of the Duke—His interest in naval and military matters—Walter Stuart—Richmond's dislike for Copenhagen—His letters to his steward at Cobham—Goods sent for from England—Richmond's addiction to drink—His financial affairs entrusted to Frances—His complete faith in her—Francis Digby—Dryden's poem on his death and Buckingham's parody—Account of the Duke's death—Arrangements for the funeral—Henshaw appointed ambassador—Charles II's. comment on his reluctance—The King's kindness to Frances—The Duke's debts—Petition of the 'Mother of the Maids'—Charles II. confers a pension on the Duchess—The Duke's body brought back to England in a Danish ship—The King of Denmark's present to Frances—The Danish Captain rewarded—The Duke's funeral—An elegy written on his death.

If the King desired this embassy to Denmark to be sumptuous and magnificent, he had chosen the right man in the Duke of Richmond, who was only too willing to create an impression of splendour consistent with his rank. The most elaborate preparations were made. A large amount of new clothes in the latest fashion were purchased by the Duke, including various garments made of fur to help him to withstand the rigours of the Northern climate.

Pains were also taken to see that his equipage should be worthy of the ' ambassador of the greatest quality that . . . England ever sent to Denmark.' New liveries were provided for all the servants, and the Duke ordered two new coaches, each with sets of harness for six horses. One was to be a great velvet coach with gold and silver fringe inside and outside, and even the less gorgeous one was to be lined with ' gold color and crimson wrought velvet.'[1]

Before he left in April 1672 he was diplomatic enough to pay a ceremonial visit to the French Ambassador and to assure him that he would always act in concert with Monsieur Terlon, the French representative at Copenhagen, and 'that in addition to the orders he had from the King his master he considered himself bound in gratitude for the favours he had received from His Majesty in France to do all that he could for his service.'[2]

Owing to calms and contrary winds the vessel carrying the Duke and his staff took nearly six weeks to reach Copenhagen, and even then Richmond would not make his public entry till some days later, when he had been able to make complete arrangements for a procession of more than usually ostentatious splendour. Henshaw, who was associated with him in the embassy, was inclined to be contemptuous

[1] Add MSS. 21,950 ff. 329, 366, etc.
[2] C.A. 103. Colbert de Croissy to Pomponne, April 11th, 1672.

La Belle Stuart 193

of this inordinate desire for display, and considered that his preparations were to 'dazeling and magnifique for that meridian.'[1] In all probability they were, for it is obvious from the Duke's subsequent comment that he had expected to find a far more cultured and fashionable Court in Copenhagen.

It has commonly been supposed that the Duke was merely a figure-head, and that the negotiations were in reality conducted by Henshaw, but the diplomatic correspondence clearly shows that this was not so,[2] although it is true that Henshaw was to a certain extent entrusted with the diplomatic secrets. This was done in case anything should happen to the Duke, and the precaution in the event proved to have been amply justified. But it was the Duke in person who treated with the Danish statesmen, and on his own confession Henshaw, though present in the room at these interviews in order to give his opinion if called upon, did not take part in the discussions, and was very often not even within earshot.[3]

Apart from the general conspiracy among his contemporaries to deny any sort of merit to the Duke of Richmond, it is difficult to say how this misapprehension as to Henshaw's real position has

---

[1] Cal. Stat. Pap. Foreign. Denmark 19. f. 121
[2] Despatches in Cal. Stat. Pap. Foreign. Denmark 19. and letters of Secretary Coventry to the envoys (Add MSS. 25,117).
[3] Cal. Stat. Pap. Foreign. Denmark 19, f. 129.

arisen. There was no manner of reason why the Duke himself should have been deemed unfitted for the task. The high offices he had filled both in Scotland and England had given him experience in such work, and the way in which he had hitherto discharged his duties had sufficiently proved his ability. His despatches from Denmark are far from being those of a fool; they show on the contrary an admirable grasp of the purposes of his mission. Henshaw himself, though he had originally doubted the Duke's capacity, was the first to give him his due. Almost as soon as they arrived, he had written to his friend Williamson: "If he continue as he has begun he will prove an extraordinary person, he has hitherto carried himself with that sobriety, prudence, and diligence that I begin to hope he may hereafter bee able to doe the King important service."[1] He was not mistaken in his estimate of Richmond's diligence; for the Duke soon threw himself into the work with such application that he even began to encroach upon the secretarial business which more properly came within Henshaw's province. Henshaw wrote to the Secretary of State, Lord Arlington, explaining the reason for the long intervals between his reports. "That which I must offer as my best excuse is the punctuall care and diligence of my Lord Duke of Richmond who hath been pleased to take on him the trouble

[1] Cal. Stat. Pap. Foreign. Denmark 19 f. 121.

La Belle Stuart

with his own hand to give your Lordship or Mr. Secretary Coventry a constant account of what hath passed here even to the smallest circumstances, so that in that affaire there hath scarse been any thing left for me to doe, unlesse I would have troubled you with repetitions, beside that for the most part my Lord Duke was able to doe it uppon better ground and information then my self; and, my Lord, if I should tell you I have been very well pleased with it, it is not that my paines were saved by it, (which I never valued) but that he might thereby the better fit himself to serve his Majesty in those employments his birth and quality require him."[1]

The Duke of Richmond's private correspondence during his embassy[2] affords a remarkably clear insight into his character and tastes, and makes it easier to understand Frances's affection for him. There appears to have been a great deal in him to like and even a little to respect. The collection consists of most of the important letters which he received together with copies of his answers. The picture of the Duke is necessarily somewhat incomplete, since he appears to have kept only those letters which contained information on some matter of importance, whether domestic, financial, or political. Personal letters from his wife, family, and friends and his answers to them are comparatively

[1] Cal. Stat. Pap. Foreign. Denmark f. 228. [2] Add MSS. 21,948.

few. But although this is a great loss it is in some measure compensated for by the fact that both sides are available of that part óf the correspondence which was deemed worthy of preservation.

One of his better qualities, which is here admirably illustrated, was his lively interest in military and naval matters. There are letters proving the care he took for the welfare of his regiment in Kent, while the documents dealing with naval matters are numerous. He corresponded with the famous shipbuilder Pett concerning his yacht, and kept himself thoroughly well informed as to the doings of the fleet. One of his correspondents on naval matters was the Duchess's brother, Walter Stuart, who, after serving in Lord Douglas's regiment in France, had now come over to England and joined the fleet as a volunteer on board the ' Montague.' The Duke had always taken a great interest in his career, and they were on very affectionate terms. ' I am sorry,' wrote Walter Stuart, ' that I heare nothing yet of your Graces returning home for I am sure that I shall find every body when I come a shoare very mallencoly for want of your good company. For my owne part I shall have the greatest reason in the world to be so, since I have ever found the greatest obligations and kindnesse from your Grace of any man alive, and therefore will find the greatest misse of your absence.'[1]

[1] Add MSS. 21,948. f. 258.

CHARLES STUART, DUKE OF RICHMOND AND LENNOX
Sir Peter Lely, Lennoxlove

Possessing, as he did, so many maritime interests, the Duke had wisely taken care always to remain friendly with the officials of the Navy Office, especially with Brouncker and Pepys. The latter in his letters to the Duke was evidently as enthusiastic in his praises of feminine beauty as he was in the more secret recesses of his own diary, for Richmond wrote to him with mock-jealousy : " Now allow me to tell you that I envy your happinesse for haveing the pleasure of soe many fine women—whilst poor I know no such thing."[1]

Richmond had not found Copenhagen as congenial as he had thought it would be. He considered the Danes dull and their women unprepossessing. To his friend, Lord Essex, who himself had formerly been English ambassador in Denmark, he wrote : " Neaver man was so weary of a place as I am of this, it being I thinke the least diverteing of any that ever I came in,"[2] and he assured Williamson that nothing should be wanting in his pains to effect what he was sent for that he might the sooner return.[3] Henshaw was as emphatic in his dislike of the Northern capital : ' Now in the pleasantest season of the yeare,' he wrote, ' this is one of the dullest places, that ever mortalls layd out their pretious minutes in.'[4]

[1] Ibid. f. 240.   [2] Stowe MSS. 200. f. 330.
[3] Cal. Stat. Pap. Foreign. Denmark 19 f. 115.
[4] Ibid. f. 154.

The part of the correspondence which reveals the Duke's most amiable characteristics is that with his agent, Jarvis Maplesden, and his steward, Roger Payne, concerning his affairs at his beloved Cobham. The best of relations subsisted between master and servants, implicit trust on the one hand and really affectionate devotion on the other. The Duke's intense love for his home is shown in these letters in which he seems to linger regretfully on such bucolic subjects as the sowing of crops in particular fields and the fencing-in of a rabbit-warren. He enquires repeatedly as to the state of his herd of deer, and is particularly anxious about the welfare of his horses and dogs. When he considered that his wife's set of grey coach-horses must be 'worn out,' he gave instructions that she was to have his own, which had by now been rested enough. Jarvis Maplesden hastened to assure his master that they had been handed over to her in the best of condition : " Concerning your Grace's old sett of coach-horses : My Lady came to Cobham Hall about the 15th of May and went away againe aboute the 10th of June, and had the Coach and 6 horses with her, which were when she received them in a good condicon ffat and faire."[1] But the Duke was not concerned only with the stables and farms at Cobham. To his servant Flexney returning from Denmark he gave

[1] Add MSS. 21,948. f. 231.

orders relating to his indoor possessions: "You must be sure to speak to Jarvis Mapleston that he takes a speciall care of my armes and swords and that he keeps them very cleane and rubs them and my books, and that a fire be made sometimes to ayer ye clossett."[1]

Richmond's amiable self-indulgence and love of comfort are delightfully shown in the lists of the things which he felt he could not do without, but had to send for from England as being unobtainable in Denmark. Among these indispensable luxuries appear sugar and spice, Cheshire cheeses, 6 pounds of Spanish tobacco, 6 pounds of Virginia Tobacco, and a gross of pipes.[2] He was evidently feeling the cold and damp of the Danish climate, as the lists also include goloshes, extra blankets, and a sable muff. Besides these he ordered a heavy coat 'lined with best grey Siberia squirrels,' because, as he said, ' without some furre here is no living.'[3]

But his chief solace and his never failing remedy against cold and boredom was, sad to say, the bottle. His bills for wine, always considerable, were still larger now, and the exigencies of ambassadorial entertainments cannot quite account for the abnormal increase. Not that he ever attempted to disguise his greatest weakness. It was well-known

[1] Add MSS. 21951. f. 40.
[2] Add MSS. 21950. f. 423.
[3] Add MSS. 21948. f. 289.

that the shortest way to his heart was through his glass. Even his sister, Lady Catherine O'Brien,[1] when she had a favour to ask of him, prepared the ground by pandering to his favourite weakness: "I have uskibath[2] redy for you when ever you will command sum;" she wrote temptingly, adding, "and if you stay all winter it will be very hollsom in that cold place."[3]

The correspondence affords complete evidence to prove that the old affection between the Duke and Duchess remained undiminished. They wrote to each other by every post, the Duke addressing his wife always as "My dear Hart," and it is significant to note how he became increasingly inclined to entrust to her the management of his interests in England. From the first he had arranged by a power of attorney that she was to receive for him the moneys accruing to him from his aulnage[4] rights, but so admirably did she acquit herself of the task that he ended by relegating financial matters almost entirely to her. "I can not soe well leave money in any hands as yours,"[5] he wrote to her, and by a second power of

---

[1] Although Lord O'Brien was a peer, his wife appears to have been universally known as Lady Catherine O'Brien and not as Lady O'Brien.

[2] i.e. from the old Irish uisge beatha—the water of life. Later called usquebaugh and now commonly known as whisky.

[3] Add MSS. 21948. f. 254.

[4] The aulnage was a duty on vendible woollen cloths.

[5] Add MSS. 21948. f. 281.

attorney arranged that the weekly payments by the Exchequer for his ambassadorial expenses were to be paid direct to her. She was rapidly becoming an astute business-woman and was indefatigable in her care for her husband's concerns, accounting to him with scrupulous care for all his money in her hands. Roger Payne was open in his admiration for her capabilities and wrote to the Duke that my Lady was 'the only instrumental cause of cleering all difficultyes in your business and the serving your Grace's interest here."[1] Richmond did his best to repay his wife by responding readily to her request to be allowed to effect improvements in the Whitehall lodgings, where she was now almost always in residence. " I hope I have not in any thing wherein I was able but complyed with your desires," he wrote to her, "and therefore I now send you an order for £500 to Mr. Clinkard." This money she was to devote to making the lodging more comfortable in any way she might wish.[2]

His implicit trust in her was not confined to financial matters, he was also sure that he might leave his honour safely in her hands, in spite of the admirers who surrounded her. One of the most importunate was Francis Digby, the younger son of the Earl of Bristol; but he was unable to turn her from her fidelity to her husband. So single-hearted, how-

[1] Add MSS. 21948. f. 287. [2] Ibid. f. 251.

ever, was his passion for her that he felt he could not bear to live without her love, and it was openly said that the gallant death he met in the naval battle against the Dutch off Southwold Bay, May the 28th, 1672, did not come to him unsought. He had never attempted to keep the secret of his hopeless passion or of his despair, and the tragic manner of his death held an appeal to the imagination of the sentimental. Dryden even felt impelled to celebrate the romance in somewhat indifferent verse.

" Farewell, fair Armida, my joy and my grief,
In vain I have loved you, and hope no relief ;
Undone by your virtue, too strict and severe,
Your eyes gave me love, and you gave me despair ;
Now call'd by my honour, I seek with content
The Fate which in pity you would not prevent :
To languish in love were to find by delay
A death that's more welcome the speediest way.

On seas, and in battles, through bullets and fire,
The danger is less than in hopeless desire ;
My death's wound you give me, tho' far off I bear
My fall from your sight, not to cost you a tear ;
But if the kind flood on a wave would convey,
And under your window my body would lay ;
When the wound on my breast you happen to see,
You'd say with a sigh, it was given by me."[1]

[1] First published in ' The Covent Garden Drollery.'

This pathetic lament had some vogue at the time, chiefly, of course, because of the circumstances which brought it forth, but it was of a nature that seemed to demand parody, and of parodists there were found not a few. The Duke of Buckingham hailed the poem with delight both as a means of venting his spleen on the poet and of getting in a back-handed gibe at the lady, who had not only once repulsed his own advances, but had also frustrated his ignoble plans for her future. In his play " The Rehearsal," which was a satire on Dryden, he produced a version of the poem supposed to have been " made by Tom Thimble's first wife, after she was dead." " But here's the conceit," says Bayes, the ludicrous poet representing Dryden in the play, " that upon his knowing she was killed by an accident, he supposes with a sigh that she died for love of him."

> " In swords, pikes, and bullets, 'tis safer to be
> Than in a strong castle remoted from thee !
> My death's bruise pray think you give me, tho' a fall
> Did give it to me, from the top of a wall :
> For then if the mote on her mud would first lay,
> And after, before you my body convey,
> The blue on my breast, when you happen to see,
> You'll say with a sigh, there's a true-blue for me."

But the Duchess was soon to receive news of a death that was bound to affect her far more than that of a rejected lover ; for in the winter her husband died at Elsinore. On the 12th of December he had gone thither to visit the English fleet, which was in those waters. The weather was severe and there was some danger that the fleet might be frozen in for the whole winter, if it did not get away speedily. The Duke sent his gentleman of the horse to Sir John Paul, the English Consul, asking his opinion as to whether it would be possible for the fleet to sail out seeing that the weather was " thick snowy and also frezing." Paul replied that it would be advisable for the fleet to sail out of the Sound as soon as the weather cleared up, and anchor further out, where the ships would be quite as safe as in the Sound and yet not run the risk of being frozen in. The advice proved excellent, for the Dutch fleet through remaining in the Sound was frozen in this same winter, as Paul himself later related with unconcealed glee. The Duke and captains determined to act upon this suggestion, and all officers proceeded straight on board as soon as the Council broke up. A little time after the Duke took it into his head that he too would go on board. He announced his intention to Paul, who did his utmost to dissuade him; but his expostulations were unavailing and only had the effect of making the Duke insist upon his coming too. The more objections Paul offered, the more obstinate the Duke became, and in the end he actually insisted upon proceeding right out to the new anchoring-place, although Paul warned him that it was not customary for any ambassador to go out of the Sound in a ship unless homeward bound, and that the Danes would probably resent his doing so. But nothing he could say was to any purpose when the Duke was in this mood. " And a little tyme efter," wrote Paul in his account of the affair, " wee went to dinner, where severall health were drunck but I cannot say to any great hight of drincking as I have seen his Grace at other tymes doe, nor to my thoughts were any of the company concerned. Its trew his grace was a littell merry but not to say much concerned. He spoke and went as well as he had never druncke nor doe I believe that he druncke 2 bottells of wine."[1]

Even after this unwontedly modest indulgence, it is scarcely to be wondered that the Duke was somewhat drowsy when he landed in the afternoon. He got into his carriage looking rather dazed, and the journey back to Elsinore began. Several times on the way back his suite became apprehensive about him, as he seemed to have lost consciousness, and when Elsinore was reached at last he was taken out of the carriage senseless and deathly pale. Nothing that the doctors could do would revive him, and finally they were forced to the conclusion that he was probably already dead when he was brought in. " They all conclude he died of a convulsion fitt," says Paul. He had evidently for some time been

[1] Cal. Stat. Pap. Foreign. Denmark. Despatch from Sir John Paul. f. 232.

subject to such attacks, for Henshaw and the Duke's physician, Dr. Taylor, admitted that several times during the summer they had given him over for dead.[1] His constitution was no doubt undermined through excessive indulgence in liquor, and it was a simple matter for Boreas to complete the work set on foot by Bacchus.

It was at once decided that the Duke's body should be sent back to England; it was accordingly embalmed, the bowels and brains being removed and buried in the Dutch church at Elsinore. A leaden coffin was ordered, but there proved to be considerable difficulty in obtaining it. " My Lord's corpse remains at Sir John Paul's at Elsinore, and this week they finish the leaden chest: about forming of which there was a great trouble, for the people of this country never saw one made of that fashion before; yet by the care and diligence of Mr. Henshaw and Dr. Taylor, and by their directions it is at last well-fitted; this chest is to be put into another covered with velvet, and so the corps shall remain there untill further order from England."[2]

If additional proof be needed that the negotiations had hitherto actually been conducted by the Duke in person, it is to be found in the fresh instructions sent out to Henshaw, ordering him to continue the work

---

[1] Ibid.
[2] Ibid. Letter from Edward Clarke to Joseph Williamson. f. 242

on the lines laid down by his predecessor.[1] The appointment came as something of a surprise to Henshaw, who had not expected to be so advanced. Truth to tell, the decision was not altogether agreeable to him, because he had hoped to be allowed to return to England to get married. When the King was told of this he remarked cynically that in his opinion " It were more reasonable for a man that had a wife to seek a foreign imployment to leave her, then having an imployment to leave that to seek a wife."[2]

With the Duke's death there perished also the last remnant of Charles II's. resentment against him. His bitterness had gradually vanished away during the last months; he had of late become far better disposed towards him, and had several times caused him to be told that he was well pleased with the way in which he was conducting the negotiations. In fulfilment of Lord Ashley's prophecy the Duke's employment had restored to him the King's trust and kindness. To the widowed Duchess Charles II. proved a good friend. Henshaw was instructed to take the utmost care of the Duke's personal property in Denmark and to see that it was restored intact to the Duchess. The King also gracefully made her a present of the valuable plate, which had been furnished out of the Jewel House for the Duke during

[1] Add MSS. 25,117. f. 74. [2] Add MSS. 25,117. f. 92.

his embassy.[1] On this subject Secretary Coventry, who was himself a great friend of the Duchess and most eager to serve her interest, wrote to Henshaw on January the 24th, 1673.[2] " My last gave you notice of the King's commands that you should take care in generall of my Lord Duke of Richmond's goods, and more particularly of the plate, and all other concerns of the Dutchesses.

I repeat it to you again to let you know that care and paines therein will be very acceptable to His Majesty, and you will besides oblige the best and most acknowledging Lady in the world, and tho her quallity is too high to make any undecent stoops for small advantages, yet the Condition my Lord hath lef her in cannot dispose her to despise such incidents as may honourably be received."

The fact of the matter was that the Duke's death had leff his widow in no very enviable position. As she had produced no heir, the titles and estates of Richmond and Lennox reverted to the King as the nearest heir male, save for the barony of Clifton which, since it could descend in the female line, passed to the Duke's sister Lady Catherine O'Brien. Cobham Hall was the only estate which was disposable in default of issue, and by her husband's will the Duchess was to have a life-interest in the

---

[1] King's Warrant Book III. 229, Add MSS. 28,074. f. 142.
[2] Add MSS. 25,117. f. 81.

estate and the house with all its contents, so long as she continued a widow. All his personal property at Whitehall consisting of jewels and furniture was, however, left to her unconditionally. But as the Duke's debts were rather considerable and his personal property would have to be realized to meet them, Frances was faced with the prospect of an existence of comparative penury. His debts in Denmark, it is true, were not very important, amounting in all to some £1500, but it was imperative that they should be settled forthwith. Henshaw wrote asking for money to pay them and requesting ' that my Lord Treasurer and my Lady Dutchesse should be put in minde how much it may bee for the King's and her advantage to agree upon some expedients to discharge all heere as soon as may be."[1]

The debts in England were much more extensive. The Duke had had a great position to keep up and had done it extravagantly, as may be judged from such accounts of his as have been preserved.[2] Enormous sums were due to jewellers, lace-makers, tailors, gold and silver fringe-makers, booksellers, and saddlers. The Duke had always allowed his bills to run on indefinitely until they assumed alarming proportions. His chemist's bill for instance had

---

[1] Cal. Stat. Pap. Foreign. Denmark 19. f. 243.
[2] Add MSS. 21,950. (*passim*).

amounted by November 1670 to no less than £406 6s. 5d. The Duke had then thought fit to pay £50 on account.[1] Bills of all kinds now came pouring in to the Duke's executors. One of the most curious applications they received was calculated to awaken strange memories in the Duchess. It was a petition from the ' Mother of the Maids,' the official chaperon at Court of the Maids of Honour. Dated March the 11th, 167$\frac{2}{3}$, it ran :[2]

" There is a custome in the Kings House that when any maide of honor maryes there a fee belongs to the Mother : which is her bed and furniture of the maid's chamber and a present from him that maryes her beside : (but I had none) which is an ill president of a great Duke.

The Duke of Richmond, marying the maide Mrs. Stuard, was desierous to let the bed stand in the roome for a littel time. The Mother gave consent to satisfie him, but finding all things laide aside, and his honour nothing, took the bed and furniture into her possession, but the Duke would needs desire the Lord Chamberlaine of the King and Lord Cornbery to desire me to deliver him the bed and furniture upon assurance of sending me £100 the next morning, which they gave me assurance should be done as I am abell to prove by wittnesses, but he hath keept the bed and furnitur all his life and never gave me

[1] Ibid. f. 259.   [2] Egerton MSS. 2435.

any satisfaction at all, so I desire the executors to take notice that I demand it as a debt due to me since His Grace has left enoufe to pay his debts; I hope they will in justice satisfie me."

Unfortunately there is no evidence to show whether this was an accurate version of the facts of the case, but if the petitioner's story be true, it is to be hoped that the executors rectified the Duke's unforgivable omission to pay his love-dues.

With the Duke's estate so seriously embarrassed Frances would have been reduced to poverty, had not Charles II. treated her with the utmost generosity. He gave her the Dukedom of Lennox and the Earldom of Darnley in life-rent,[1] and, what is more, adhered to this arrangement, for, when some years later he granted the Dukedom of Lennox to his son by Louise de Keroualle, it was 'under such reservations as may render valid the former grant to the Duchess.'[2] He also continued to give her the aulnage rights granted to the late Duke,[3] and bestowed on her a pension of £1000 a year to be paid quarterly out of the London Excise.[4] He remained always scrupulously regardful of her interests, and,

---

[1] Cal. Stat. Pap. Dom. 1673 'Earl of Kincardine to the Commissioners of the Treasury in Scotland.' Cal. Stat. Pap. Scotland, Warrant Book II. 374.

[2] Cal. Stat. Pap. Scotland, Warrant Book VI., 90.

[3] King's Warrant Book III.

[4] Ibid. 350.

though such pensions were often allowed to fall into arrears, he seems to have made every effort to see that hers at least was paid regularly. A special arrangement was made whereby, failing the London Excise, her pension was to be paid out of any money in the Exchequer.[1] As evidence of his continued attention to this matter it is worth mentioning that, when funds were very low in October 1675, he caused the letter directing the payment of a quarter of her pension to be endorsed 'By the King's special command.'[2] in order to ensure priority of payment to her before other applicants.

Although the Duke of Richmond had died in December 1672, his body did not reach England till the following September. Various causes had contributed to the delay, including an exchange of compliments between the Kings of England and Denmark when the latter offered to provide a Danish ship to escort the corpse of His Britannic Majesty's Ambassador Extraordinary back to England. Charles II. was graciously pleased to accept the offer; but for some time it seemed that the King of Denmark had only made the suggestion by way of politeness, for nothing was done, and Henshaw had to be instructed to put some courteous pressure on the Danes before the promised vessel was forthcoming.[3]

[1] Add MSS. 28,074. f. 224.
[2] Treasury Minute Book V., 59.
[3] Add MSS. 25,117.

La Belle Stuart 213

However, in the end all was satisfactorily settled and the Duke's body came back to England in a ship of the country to which he had been accredited. A great deal of trouble was taken to decorate the ship in a manner which the taste of the time considered appropriate to her mournful errand. Not only was her hull painted an unrelieved black, but she was also furnished with black sails.[1] Henshaw announced the impending departure in a despatch of August the 2nd, and mentioned that the King of Denmark was sending the Duchess his own miniature set with diamonds, being the present which he had intended to give the Duke on the termination of his embassy.[2] This gift the Duchess actually received, as it appears that she found some difficulty in inditing her letter of thanks. She sent a draft of it to Coventry asking him to peruse it and make any necessary corrections. ' I have as neer as my poor capasety will allow, and my bad french, taken the sense of what you were pleased to advise, but yet I fear it is not well enough (even for a Northern Countrey) therefore once more I do again implore your aide in this. . .'[3] Either this was undue modesty on the part of the Duchess or else long lack of practice had made her forget her French, for when

---

[1] Hist. MSS. Comm. Report. 12. Ap. 7. ' MSS. of S. H. Le Fleming at Rydal Hall. f. 103. Newsletter.

[2] Cal. Stat. Pap. Foreign. Denmark. f. 289.

[3] Original letter in the Collection of the Marquess of Bath, K.G. at Longleat.

she first came to England she had spoken it as well as or even better than her mother-tongue, at least so says Gramont, and he was never inclined to give too favourable an opinion of her accomplishments.

The captain of the Danish ship, which escorted the Duke's body back to England, was liberally rewarded for his services; he received £150 or more from the executors, a chain and medal worth as much from the King, and from the widowed Duchess 'a rich belt, and sword, of massy gold to the value of about £100.[1]

The body was landed at Gravesend, the nearest port to the late Duke's home, and some ten days later a melancholy procession of barges made its way up the river to Westminster. The barge which bore the coffin was draped with velvet. On the evening of September the 19th the funeral took place at Westminster Abbey with a pompous parade that would have delighted the heart of the Duke. Most of the nobility attended, and the Knights of the Garter, wearing the Collars of their Order, came to pay their last respects. The chief mourner was the Earl of Norwich, Earl Marshall, cousin german of the deceased Duke, and the pall-bearers were the Earl of Arran, Lord Buckhurst, Lord Annesley, and Lord Howard. The body was interred under the monument of the Duke's great-uncle, Ludovic,

---

[1] Add MSS. 25,117. f. 141.

La Belle Stuart 215

Duke of Richmond and Lennox, 'which done, Garter Principal King of Arms proclaimed his Grace's stile and titles, and so the solemnity ended.'[1]

It can be imagined how painful such ceremonies must have been to Frances, taking place so long after her husband's death, and reopening a wound that the flight of time might have begun to heal. The Duke's death was made the subject of a lugubrious elegy,[2] composed by some poetaster and hawked about the streets. It was printed on a broadsheet adorned with a gloomy border of skeletons, hour-glasses, spades, picks, shrouds, and other appropriate emblems of Death and the undertaker. The Duchess's grief is thus portrayed by the anonymous poet:

> " Grief's sables now surround the gloomy room,
> And sighs like incense cloud it with perfume
> From her sweet breath; whilst her two panting breasts
> Like little mournful birds droop in their nests:
> The funeral tapers burn, but with dim light,
> Naught but her eyes, beneath her vail, shines bright.
>
> .   .   .   .   .   .
>
> Let none into her presence dare t'intrude
> Once to disturb her graceful solitude:
> She needs none of your help, let her alone,
> The turtle by herself loves to bemoan."

[1] London Gazette, September 22nd, 1673. No. 818.
[2] There is a copy of this broadsheet in the Luttrell Collection. British Museum).

CHAPTER IX

Strained relations between Frances and Lady Catherine O'Brien—Their letters to Lord Essex—Frances sells her life-interest in Cobham Hall—Rumour that she is married to Lord Mulgrave—The Northumberland claimant in the House of Lords—The Duchess of Richmond's finances—The affair of Jack How—Triumphant vindication of the Duchess of Richmond's virtue—Charles II's. friendship with Frances—Her skill in dancing—Her fondness for the theatre—Nathaniel Lee—Frances and her cousin, Lord Blantyre—Letter to him—Death of Charles II.—More letters to Blantyre.

When a man dies leaving a wife but no children, the disposition of his estate is often a cause for acute heartburning between his relations, the eventual heirs, and the widow, whom they are inclined to regard as a stranger usurping what in their own opinion should more properly belong to themselves. This was so in a marked degree in the case of the life-interest in Cobham Hall left to Frances by her husband. She and the Duke's sister, Lady Catherine O'Brien, had never at the best of times been disposed to like one another; but now, when Lady Catherine openly showed her resentment on hearing that Frances was still to keep possession of the ancestral home of the Richmonds, their indifference to each other seemed likely to develop into open hostility. The position of the Duke's executors was most unenviable. The actual business of winding up the estate was chiefly entrusted to Sir Charles Bickerstaffe, but to Lord Essex, who luckily had been trained in diplomacy from his youth up, fell the delicate task of attempting to compose the differences between the two ladies, with both of whom he was on very friendly terms. It was only the knowledge that his great friendship for both would make him scrupulously fair in his judgment that restrained both the ladies from telling him exactly what each thought of the other. But even when Lady Catherine was at her most querulous, she took care to remain carefully moderate in her language about Frances. Having occasion to send Lord Essex a document to sign for her in December 1673, she took the opportunity to air her grievances: 'My Lord, att the same time that I begg your Excellency's pardon for this trouble, I must also importune you to give me leave (within a few dayes) to present the hardship of my condition in relation to my deare brother Richmond's estate, which by different interests and the jarring opinion of lawyers is likely to be ruined. I complaine not of my sister Richmond; her demands are (att least her Counsell tells her they are) very legall, but other interests have so interwoven themselves with hers that I feare the beauty of the house and park att Cobham (the delight of my dear relations) will be utterly defaced, and the estate prejudiced many thousand pounds. And all this to force conditions upon me neither advantageous to my sister, profitable to the estate, nor honourable to the living or dead.'[1]

Frances, who hated wrangling and desired nothing more than to be left in peace, did her best to conciliate her sister-in-law, and some sort of a temporary accommodation was patched up in the following March. In a letter to Lord Essex she showed her intense relief, though she too was quite unable to conceal the sharp claws beneath the velvet paw. ' I shall not, my Lord, trouble you with an impertenent account of what has passed betwixt my sister Katherine and me, because it is not worth your knowledge (in any sense it can be taken) or indeed materiell (I thinke hardly to her selfe), and what ever is so in the maine buissness I am sure Sir Henry Capell does very perfectly aquant you with. Therefore, my Lord, I shall only give you this farther trouble now, to tell you how glad I am that afffter all these storms in which I have bine tost both by my sister and such engins as she has yett on worke I am lickly now to have some rest and comfort of my life by a happy conclusion of our greatest differences. All now will depend on yor Excellency's saffety (and the other Executors) which I am yet more concerned for then my own, and I make it heere my request that you will waigh that above anything

[1] Stowe MSS. 203. f. 317.

else. Nay though I should suffer by it in my fortune, for then perhaps my mind would be in pain, and that is much the worst of ills.'[1]

A year or so later, in 1677, to be precise, the best possible solution of all these difficulties was found, when Frances agreed to sell her life-interest in Cobham Hall to Lady Catherine's husband, Lord O'Brien, as trustee for their son, Donatus, the eventual heir. The Duchess received £3,800 for surrending her rights. This arrangement met with the approval of both parties; Lady Catherine wrote to Essex expressing her own satisfaction and telling him that Frances also had professed herself content with the settlement.[2]

At the time when this occurred John Verney, writing to his brother Sir Ralph, made a singular statement: ' The Duchess of Richmond hath lately sold her interest in Cobham to Lord O'Brian, soe 'tis believed she will suddenly own her marriage to the Lord Mulgrave.[3] The impassioned poem which Mulgrave had addressed to Frances during her husband's lifetime shows that he had even then been her fervent admirer, but he appears now to have resumed his pursuit of her with more honourable intentions. Rumour at least credited him with being a suitor for her hand, and a ludicrous incident which

[1] Stowe MSS. 201. f. 223.
[2] Stowe MSS. 211 . f. 108. Letter of February 13th, 1677.
[3] Original letter among the Verney Papers at Claydon House.

occurred at the end of this year in all probability tended to increase popular belief in the truth of the report. When Joscelin Percy, Earl of Northumberland, died in 1670, the earldom had become extinct; but a claimant had arisen in one James Percy, an eccentric trunk-maker, who claimed to be cousin and next heir-male of the late Earl. This individual one day made his way into the House of Lords when the King and the Duke of York were present, and informed His Majesty that he came to desire to be allowed to sit there as a Plantagenet. Always ready for a jest, the King allowed him to dilate upon his pretensions, while the Lord Chancellor, entering also into the spirit of the joke, affected to give the King solemn warning that he must take care how he countenanced such claims, lest this heir of an ancient line should prove to possess a better title than the Duke of York to succeed him on the throne. To this the claimant in all seriousness answered that he aimed not at the Crown, but that his request to the King was to command the younger Duchess of Richmond to marry him. This extraordinary and unexpected demand caused immense amusement among those present, and the King laughingly declared that to grant such a petition was not in his power, and he would have to trust to his own attractions to conquer the lady's heart and win her hand. Upon this the disappointed suitor pointed dramatically to Lord Mulgrave, and cried: ' No, that fellow

LORD MULGRAVE

[face p. 220

there will hinder me !' This outburst provoked still more merriment among their lordships, and one may depend upon it that the unfortunate Mulgrave was most unmercifully chaffed by his peers.[1]

There does not, however, seem to be any real evidence that the Duchess ever seriously contemplated marrying Lord Mulgrave, much less that she was clandestinely married to him. He may have made her a proposal of marriage, but, if he did, she refused him. Even if he was disappointed at the time, he did not prove inconsolable ; for he married three times before he closed his eventful career.

Frances never married again. With her distaste for the realities of love there was little to tempt her to do so. She had all that she wanted in life, an illustrious position, the friendship of her sovereigns, universal admiration for her beauty, and, thanks to the King's generous treatment of her on the death of her husband, an adequate income, which through her own prudent management was continually increasing. In 1677 she obtained an additional annuity of £1000 out of the Hereditary Excise of Middlesex, Kent, Surrey, and Essex, by selling to the King her rights in the duchy of Aubigny, which by arrangement with Louis XIV. was transferred to the new Duke of Richmond and Lennox, Charles II's. son by Louise de Keroualle.

Now at long last the world was beginning to

[1] Hist. MSS. Comm. Report. Rutland MSS. II. 42. Viscountess Campden to Lord Roos, at Belvoir Castle, December 4th, 1677.

believe that the Duchess of Richmond was really as chaste and as virtuous as she claimed to be. The fact that, though she held a prominent position at Court, she was spared by the satirists who delighted to shower their pointed barbs upon the Duchesses of Cleveland and Portsmouth, and most of the other well-known beauties at Court, shows that on the whole her character was respected.[1] The only allusions to her discoverable in the mass of ribald lampoons that were so characteristic of the period, consist in intimations that her day was over, as in the following lines from a pasquinade on the King's mistresses entitled 'Cullen with his flock of Misses.' 1679.[2]

> "This hour from French intrigues ('tis said)
> He'll clear his Council and his bed.
> Portsmouth he vouchsafes to know
> Was the cast whore of Count de Loe.
> She must return and sell her place;
> Buyers (you see) flock in apace.
> Silence i' th' Court being once proclaim'd,
> In steps fair Richmond once so fam'd:
> She offers much, but was refus'd
> And of miscarriages accus'd.
> Nor would his Majesty accept her
> At thirty, who at fifteen left her;
> She blusht, and modestly withdrew."

[1] Among the MSS belonging to the Duke of Rutland at Belvoir Castle there is an obscene poem about certain widows including the Duchess of Richmond, but, although this may have been handed about at Court, it does not seem ever to have been published.

[2] Poems on Affairs of State, Vol. I. 132.

Such scurrilous gibes referring to her past could not injure the Duchess, and she ignored them, but if anyone dared to go further and make insinuations against her present virtue, she was up in arms at once, and would fight valiantly for her honour. A certain 'young amorous spark of the Court,' one Jack How, took it into his head to fall in love with her, and openly declared his passion.[1] But the Duchess would have none of him, and rejected his addresses with scorn. Her coldness and contempt made the young man vindictive; he began to spread abroad reports of how he had been granted her favours, and offered to prove his assertions by means of several impassioned letters he claimed to have received from her. Frances was filled with indignation at these base calumnies, and determined to revenge herself upon her slanderer. She went to the King and demanded that an inquiry should be held into How's allegations, and that he should be forced to produce the letters he pretended to have received from her. His Majesty had by now come to realize that Frances was obsessed with the unfamiliar idea that chastity was the chiefest of all virtues, and that she must in consequence be humoured on the subject of her reputation. He accordingly acceded to her desire, and with all due solemnity referred the weighty matter to a Court of Honour, consisting of

[1] Sidney Correspondence. Letters to Henry Sidney from Mr. Mountstevens and the Dowager Lady Sunderland, Sept. 2nd, 1679.

some of the more illustrious members of the Privy Council. The Duke of Monmouth, the Earls of Halifax and Essex, and Lord Sunderland had the honour to be chosen to conduct the enquiry. When Jack How was brought before them it was found that all his boasted evidence consisted in a single letter. The noble lords were inclined to be suspicious even of this, but wishing to be scrupulously impartial to both sides, they referred the matter to a higher authority, the very fountain of justice itself. If they had been merely suspicious, His Majesty was quite convinced that the letter was a forgery, and unhesitatingly declared that he could himself swear that it was written neither in the Duchess of Richmond's style nor in her handwriting. The upshot of it was that Mr. Jack How was informed that his presence at Court would no longer be tolerated, while the Duchess of Richmond came through the trial with her honour triumphantly vindicated.

Whether it was because Charles had at last fathomed the peculiarities of the Duchess of Richmond's character, or because he no longer found her attractive, he had by now entirely abandoned all thought of making her his mistress. His feelings for her now were merely those of a friend. Since she had sold her interests in Cobham Hall, Frances lived at her lodgings in Whitehall whenever the Court was in London. Court life was very congenial to her, and she threw herself with great zest into every diversion that offered itself. She took a prominent part in all the masquerades, and was an honoured guest at all the most fashionable supper-parties. At balls she was in great demand, being accounted one of the best dancers in England. According to Courtin there were but few really good dancers at the English Court, the Duchess of Richmond, Princess Mary, the Duke of York's elder daughter, and the Countess of Derby being almost the only ones who could be considered as good as the best dancers in France. The state of dancing among English men was still more lamentable. In the French Ambassador's opinion there were only two who were really expert, the King and the Duke of Monmouth.[1] And yet the general lack of skill must have been due to a natural incapacity, since there was no lack of practice. Balls were given by someone or other at Court almost every day. The account of one of these given by the Duchess of Portsmouth reveals a supper arrangement that would scarcely have been expected to appeal to the Court of Charles II. After the guests had danced French dances in the Gallery until 11 o'clock they proceeded to supper, which was served at two big tables, one for the ladies, and the other for the men ! After this segregated repast a return was made to the gallery, where the company danced English country dances till three o'clock in the morning.[2]

[1] C.A. 120. Courtin to Louis XIV. November 26, 1676.
[2] C.A. 120. Courtin to Louis XIV. December 17, 1676.

The theatre continued to be one of the favourite diversions at Court. The Queen frequently attended with all her ladies. Frances had always been fond of the theatre, and her illustrious position now gave her an opportunity to extend her patronage to struggling dramatists. One whom she especially favoured was Nathaniel Lee, whose benefit-night she with characteristic good nature ensured of success by being present herself and persuading the Duchess of York, Mary of Modena, to accompany her. The exalted company proved an added attraction : the theatre was packed, and the financial result was most gratifying to the dramatist. He repaid his debt to the Duchess of Richmond by dedicating to her his ' Theodosius, or the Force of Love,' which was produced for the first time at Dorset Garden in 1680. The Dedication was flamboyant even for Lee, who had a reputation for indulging in unrestrained panegyric. ' My Genius, Madam, was your favourite when the Poet was unknown, and openly receiv'd your smiles before I had the honour to pay your Grace the most submissive gratitude for so illustrious a protection. To let the world to know that you do not think it beneath you to be officiously good, you brought Her Royal Highness just at the exigent of time, whose single presence on the Poet's Day is a subsistence for him all the year after.' Fulsome phrase follows fulsome phrase. The Duchess's ' particular goodness, and innate sweetness, merely for the sake of doing well' are extolled, as is her 'extraordinary love for heroick poetry.' 'Something there is in your mien so much above that we vulgarly call *charming*, that to me it seems adorable, and your presence almost divine.' He calls her 'Your Grace, who is the most beautiful idea of Love and Glory,' and assures her that merely to behold her 'is to make prophets quite forget their heaven, and bind the poets with eternal rapture.' Admiration of this kind was nectar to Frances. All through her life she could never be sated with it. The extravagant phrases of 'Dedicating Lee,'[1] which would have amused or disgusted others, were regarded by her merely as tributes justly due to her exceptional charm and beauty. The fervent admiration which had been showered on her all her life had endowed her with a dispassionate conviction of her own perfections that was so intense as to transcend mere conceit. The guileless sincerity of her belief in her own beauty preserved her from most of the faults which usually go with vanity, and she was altogether free from selfishness and arrogance. With the passing of years the light-hearted frivolity that had obscured her good sense in her childhood, and had led so many people astray in their estimates of her, entirely vanished, and her true character was at last revealed. And a thoroughly Scottish character it was, in spite of her

[1] This name is given to him in 'A Satyr on the poets' in Poems on Affairs of State II. 143.

upbringing in France and her long residence in England ! The racial characteristics of that people seem to be as ineradicable and as insusceptible to changes of climate and conditions as those of the Jews ! Caution and common sense were in Frances Stuart's blood ; she never allowed herself to be carried away by impulse, but carefully and coolly weighed her every action. Yet hers was not a hard nature ; her gentleness and generosity were universally acknowledged. But her kind actions were never careless, the result of that sentimental kind of charity which does not know its own object ; they were always the outcome of deep consideration and were based on a certainty that they were deserved. Truly, that nature is far from contemptible which regards its generosity as no more than justice.

Nowhere, perhaps, is the Duchess of Richmond's character more clearly illustrated than in her correspondence[1] with her cousin, Alexander Stuart, 5th Lord Blantyre. When this young man had succeeded his father he had written to her tendering his humble duty, but he had not borne out his early promise, and his opposition to the royal policy in Scotland had caused her to view him with some coldness. Consequently when he wrote again in 1684 asking for her good offices with the King, her reply[2] was inclined to be somewhat stern.

[1] Lennoxlove Papers. [2] Ibid.

Whitehall, August the 5th.

My Lord

I receeved two of yours, in which you desired me to represent you to his Majesty as one that was well affected both to him and his government, and sayed withall that the Chancelor then in being (which was the Earle of Aberdeene) would second me in it; therefore as long as he was in England, I expected still when he would lett me heere from him as to your Lordship's concerns, and concluding likewise that what should come from such a great statesman, and one too in the post that he was then, would have had a great and considerable inflewence as to the doeing you servis; but instead of that I never soe much as saw my Lord Aberdeene all the while he was heere, nor heard one word from him in any kind; but I hope notwithstanding he kept his word with you, and then you will not need the small servis I am able to do you, if I were in the way of doeing it, which God knows I am not for many reasons, and perticulierly in that I have never bine at Windsor but one day all this whole sumer, and then I had no opertunity neyther of speaking to the King; but when soeere I have I'll lett his Majesty and his Royal Highness both know what letters I had from my Lord of Blantyre, for I must confess the last time I heard them name you twas much to my trouble, for twas to tell me how ill my cossen had behaved himselfe in the Parliament, which meethought was a strange and a sad heering of a subject but more espetially of a Stuart : that name, my Lord, I hope (which you have the honor to bear) will putt you often in mind of your duty to your King, and both your consiance and honour will for the future make you so abhor any consill which may be contrary to that, as never to look on anyone heereaffter to be your friend that shall give you advise contrary to that which now comes most cordially from

Your affectionat cossen and humble servante, F. Lennox and Richmond.[1]

It is not to be wondered at that the Duchess chose to be cautious in this matter ; for, although her intense pride in her Stuart ancestry made her naturally anxious to do all that she could to advance the fortunes of the present head of her branch of the family, she scarcely knew the young man, and had so far seen little reason to believe that he would prove deserving of any efforts she might make on his behalf. It is, indeed, much to her credit that she was prepared to give him her aid, if he would declare his contrition for his previous misbehaviour. Blantyre must have thought he deserved her strictures ; he does not seem to have resented the severe tone of her letter, and later on he wrote to her again expressing

[1] When writing letters to Scotland Frances invariably put her Scottish title first.

his penitence for his opposition to the royal policy in the last Parliament and requesting her to remove the bad impressions it had caused in the King's mind. Henceforward, he declared, he would prove a loyal and dutiful subject. Frances was now satisfied as to the sincerity of his intentions, and determined to speak to the King on his behalf, but she was ill and confined to the house when his letter arrived, and so had to postpone doing him this service.

But she was not destined ever to see the King again. Although he had seemed of late to be in excellent health, he was suddenly seized on February the 2nd with an apoplectic fit of such severity that he would undoubtedly have died at that moment, if he had not been promptly let blood by Dr. King, one of his physicians who happened to be present. The doctor's action, imperative though it was, was contrary to all etiquette, as he ought to have waited until the other royal physicians had arrived before doing anything at all. The consequences might have been most serious for him, but fortunately the Privy Council approved of his action, and in appreciation of his services granted him a free pardon—and £1000, which he never received. But although the King's life had been saved for the moment it was only a temporary respite, for he soon grew worse again. After lingering for a few days more in great pain, at half past eleven in the morning of Friday

February 6th, 1685, he died, fortified with the rites of the Roman Catholic Church. He received the last sacrament at the hands of the Jesuit, Father Huddleston, whom he had first met in his wanderings after the defeat of Worcester.

Even though Frances had never loved the King, his death cannot have failed to cause her deep emotion. It would have been impossible for her to regard with indifference the passing away of one who had played so prominent a part in her life. Strongly as she had resented the unworthy advances he had once made to her, yet she could not but admit that he had at least shown that his passionate pursuit of her was inspired by a real love and not by a mere transient desire. She knew that, though he had tried to make her his mistress, he had been prepared to make her his Queen had it been possible. Moreover the faults had not all been on his side, and when she reflected upon her own behaviour during those first years at Court she cannot have satisfied herself that she was altogether free from reproach. She had not attempted to stifle the King's infatuation at its birth; she had deliberately led him on ; she had not repelled his pressing advances with indignation, she had put them off gently and guilefully in order that he might not be so disheartened as to abandon his suit. But the wrongs they had done each other had been forgiven long ago, and Frances could now look back on a period during which the King had succeeded by his kindness and generosity in proving to her that a very real and lasting affection had sprung up from the ruins of his former love. By his death she had lost one of her best and truest friends.

Some weeks after the King's death Frances wrote again to her cousin :[1]

Whitehall, March the 16th.

My Lord

When I receaved yours (in which you desired me to speake to His Majesty of you and to indeaver to remove the bad impressions which your behavoir in the last parliment had so unhappyly caused) I was then sick and kept my chamber for some time, which hindered me then from doing as you desiered, and in very few days afster I went abrod, and intended to have spoke both to his lait Majesty and this our present King, that most deplorable misfortune happed off the lait King's sickness and death, which putt such a strang consternation amongh us, and struck soe deep a sadness in every body's heart, espetially on the King his royall brother, as twas not proper, nor indeed possible to speak to him of any buissness, altho I had a great deale of my own to have minded if I could have minded any. Then I have bine sick again and forced to keepe my chamber for some weeks since the King's death, and am now

[1] Lennoxlove Papers.

but laitly come out of it. I heer, my Lord, that my Lord Chancelor and my Lord Treasurer of Scotland are arrived heere, and meethinks it shoud be much more proper for such wise and great men to speak for you and to give the King some good imprestions of you then a woman can, espetially such a one as knows you but little notwithstanding the neer relation is betwixt us ; I can not doubt, my Lord, but that you are your selfe of the same opinon, and that you have allready bine so prudent as to have ingaged eyther one or both of these our great men to recommend you to his Majesty as one that is resolved to shew your self upon all occasions a true and loyall subject, besides theer is now to be soe soon a parliment in Scotland, as twill be an eaysy matter for you your self to lett the King see that you are now become indeed the man you profess to be, and when, my Lord, you shall have done that, t'will become your freinds much better to speak prayses of you ; and I am confident who so ever shoud now tell the King how loyall you are and how dutyfull a subject you meane to be, hee would answer that now there woud quickly be a proufe of it, meaning the Parliment which is to be conveaned in Scotland. You may see, my Lord, by this letter that I take the liberty you gave me of writing freely my mind, nor coud I indeed have given my brother better advise were he liveing and in your circumstances.

But notwithstanding I have told you of so much a better way of recomending your self to His Majesty's good opinon you will have me to say any thing of you, I will be very ready to do it afster the parliment is up again and that I shall have had from your good deportment there so just and reasonable a ground for my speaking advantagiously of you, which is the thing I shall allways have a great desire to doe as beeing

        My Lord
    Your humble servante
    and affectionat cousine
    F. Lennox and Richmond.

In his answer to this letter Blantyre seemed so grateful for her advice and so sincere in his promises of loyalty that her next letter to him was rather less severely worded.

                Whitehall, May the 2nd, 1685.
My Lord

I am very glad to heer that you continew still in the same good resolutions of serveing his Majesty, and in that way which most becomes an honest man, a good subiect, and a Stuart. I have, my Lord, according to your desire, wrot to my Lord Advocate, and I dare presume to say that you will find him very kind to you, and most cordiall and freindly in his advise. I did not speak of you, my

Lord, to my Lord Chancelor when he was in England, because I had not the opertunity, for he had perpetuall buissness with the King while he was heere, though, notwithstanding, he did me the favour to come twice to my lodgings, but I had the missfortune to be then from home ; but as I take it, my Lord, 'tis now at this time in your own hands to recommend yourselfe, both to my Lord Chancelor and every other honest loyall person, by your behaviour in Parliment, which I cannot now doubt of its being what it ought to be ; and that all the good fortune immaginable may follow it is the hearty wishes of, my Lord,

Your faithful humble servante
and affectionat coussin
F. Lennox and Richmond.

If Frances had really been as foolish and as brainless as she was thought to be when she first came to Court, it is difficult to believe that she could all at once have developed the common sense and perspicacity which now guided all her actions. Such qualities as these do not spring up suddenly from nowhere ; their elements at least must always have been latent in her character. It is surely reasonable to believe that Frances never was a fool, and that beneath her apparent artlessness she had always possessed a clear head and a well-balanced mind. If this be conceded, it at once becomes easier to account for certain incidents in her career which are otherwise inexplicable. From her first appearance at Court a succession of difficulties had beset her, and from them all she had emerged triumphant and unscathed. The efforts of statesmen and diplomatists to involve her in political intrigues had somehow been frustrated; the sinister designs of Buckingham had been repeatedly foiled; the King's attempts to make her his mistress had been unavailing. Her immunity had not been achieved by sheer good luck but by her own prudent handling of most delicate situations.

When Pepys called Frances Stuart 'a cunning slut,' he was far nearer the truth than Gramont with his talk of her childishness and stupidity. The fact that even people who knew her well did not realize how much her own personality counted for is perhaps the most subtle tribute that her cleverness ever received.

CHAPTER X

The Duchess of Richmond's deposition on the birth of the Prince of Wales—Fireworks in St. James's Park—The Revolution—Frances withdraws from Society—Her ill-health—Her pension no longer paid— Petitions to William III. and Queen Anne—Her affairs in Scotland entrusted to Blantyre—Her correspondence with him—Her death—The Richmond tomb—The waxen effigy—Frances leaves a considerable fortune—The 'Cat' legend exploded—Minor bequests—The legacy of Lennoxlove—Sale of her pictures and jewels—Purchase of estates in Scotland—Lennoxlove Frances Stuart's real monument—Relics of her there—Her watch—Conclusion.

Although Lord Blantyre may have been sincere at the time in his protestations of loyalty to the King and in his promises to serve him, he was soon to find that his conscience revolted against the far-reaching political and religious changes, which James II. showed himself determined to force upon the country. Accordingly, when William of Orange appeared as a champion of the Protestant faith and constitutional government, Blantyre became a staunch adherent of his, and even gave him active support by raising a regiment. What the Duchess of Richmond thought of his behaviour is not recorded; but it is likely that her correspondence with her cousin came to an abrupt end, for she herself remained loyal to the King. She had never been

La Belle Stuart

interested in politics, but, if she had any views on such questions at all, as a Catholic and a Stuart she in all probability approved of the King's efforts to establish an autocracy and lead all England once again into the fold of the Holy Roman Church.

The Duchess of Richmond should have attended at the birth of the Prince of Wales, but she was not yet dressed when she was informed that the Queen was in labour, and although she made all the haste she could, the child had already been born when she arrived.[1] Later on when sinister rumours got abroad and the King's enemies openly expressed their belief that no child had been born, she was one of those called before the Privy Council to swear that the Queen had actually been enceinte. By so doing she incurred the opprobrium of the Protestant party:

' Rich-d and Li-d, and brave Ma-all,
 Tho' not at Labour, they believe it all;
 And fain would be believed; if these Tools
 By swearing falsely could make us such Fools:
 They give such Demonstrations, that do lye
 As much aside, as they do Modesty.[2]

---

[1] " Depositions taken the 22nd, of October 1688 before the Privy-Council and Peers of England; relating to the Birth of the Prince of Wales. Published by His Majesty's Special Command."

[2] ' The Deponents '. ' Poems on Affairs of State '. Vol. III. 262. The ladies referred to in these lines are, according to the official ' Depositions,' Frances, Duchess of Richmond and Lennox, Charlotte, Countess of Lichfield, and Anne, Countess of Marischal.

On July the 17th 1688, when an elaborate display of fireworks was given in St. James's Park to celebrate the birth of the Prince of Wales, Frances invited a party to witness the scene from her house. Among those present was the Earl of Clarendon, formerly Lord Cornbury, with whom and with his brother, Lawrence, Earl of Rochester, she had always remained very friendly.[1]

A month or so later those events occurred which drove James II. from the throne and placed William and Mary there in his stead. In view of the sentiments which Frances had expressed in her letters to Blantyre some years before it may be considered somewhat surprising that she did not think fit to follow her King into exile. But, as a matter of fact, those who actually left the country were comparatively few; many, who in their hearts were faithful to King James, remained in England in expectation of his eventual return, and in the meantime outwardly acquiesced in the Revolution settlement. Frances may even have felt that Blantyre had been right, for certainly her greatest friends, Lords Clarendon and Bath, whose counsel she was most wont to seek, had both in the end reluctantly become convinced that the interests of the kingdom demanded the deposition of James. But whatever may have been her opinions Frances

[1] Clarendon & Rochester Correspondence. Diary of Henry, Earl of Clarendon.

did not care to proclaim them abroad. She withdrew herself entirely from social activities of any kind, and led a very retired life, which, owing to the delicate state of her health, she was enabled to do without exciting comment.

James II. had continued Charles II's. kindness in seeing that her pension was regularly paid to her, but after the Revolution it was no longer paid. In 1692[1] the Duchess petitioned William III. that the arrears might be paid to her; but he replied that he regretted that there was no money in the Exchequer, as the revenue had been anticipated owing to the War. She sent in another 'memorial'[2] a few years later intimating that now there was peace the former excuse could no longer be given, but apparently no notice was taken of her request, for she renewed her petition on the accession of Queen Anne. Anne was more kindly disposed towards her; she replied that, though it was impossible to pay the arrears, the annuity should henceforward be paid regularly.

Frances was not so dependent on this source of income as she had been when it was first granted, for by careful businesslike management her estate had grown considerably. During the last few years of her life her health grew rapidly worse. She

[1] Treasury Papers. Vol. 17. (Feb. 1692.)
[2] Lennoxlove Papers. Draught of the Duchess of Richmond's 'Memoriall'.

suffered from sciatica, and the violent headaches, which she had been subject to even as a young girl, were more frequent now.[1] She entrusted[2] the management of her affairs in Scotland more and more to Blantyre, in whom she now had the utmost confidence. She corresponded with him about her affairs, and everywhere are discernible traces of her old firmness and common sense. She refused, for instance, to entertain Blantyre's suggestion that she should go to law with the heirs of one Enterkin, who for his own benefit had sold property belonging to the Duchy of Lennox to the value of £60, declaring that so small a matter was not worth either the money or trouble that would have to be spent upon it. Nor would she brook any interference from the Duke of Lennox, who also claimed to have an interest in the affair. 'By no meanes will I enter into that sute, lett the young Duke of L: be doing as he pleases with that, and all the rest when my bones shall be at rest; but in the meane time I conceive he has nothing to do with that or any other part of my estate. Nor will I allow of his being consuted in any thing that is my concern (and mine only for the time that God shall be pleased to lett me live in this world).'[3]

She was ever unwilling to be imposed upon by

[1] Lennoxlove Papers.
[2] Ibid.
[3] Lennoxlove Papers. May, 3rd, 1698.

La Belle Stuart

servants or dependents, and the following passage referring to her agent Hugh is characteristic of her. ' Hugh has not yet writ me word to Gray, as he told your Lordship he would do, about the account of what was done in my affayrs at Dunbarton ; nor will he send up his accounts of money that is in his hands of mine. He has never cleered any with me since Enterkine dyed, and I know he has since that received several summes from my vassells ; the which I expect an exact account of, and will have it too, or els put an other agent to serve me in his place, who shall account for every penny. For what I give, I give, but I will not have people to be theyr own carvers out of my purse. When you shall see him, my Lord, I desire you will be pleased to tell him so.'[1]

Frances was no mere blusterer, when she said a thing like that she meant it, and, since Hugh was foolish enough to disregard this very definite warning, he was summarily dismissed.[2] Such qualities as these are more calculated to win admiration than affection, so it is pleasant to find Frances showing more generous qualities in the same letters. ' I wish you joy, My Lord, of your nephew's marriage, and by the young lady's preetyness and descreet behavoir when I saw her, I do not doubt but she will make him happy. I have given my cousin the best advise

[1] Lennoxlove Papers. August 21st, 169(8).   [2] Ibid.

I am capable off; he promises to follow it and to be a very good husband. He told me too that he had taken care to have the duzen pound of chocolate I sent to my Lady Blantyre putt up in a lattin[1] box, which was, as I told him, the only sure way to keepe it from wett or dampness, eyther of which would spoyle it quit. I hope it is gott safe and well to your Lady's hands, and that she will like it so well as to command more of it.'[2] A few months later she writes rather disappointedly ' I fear she did not like the chocolate I sent her, because she does not command more.'[3] A passage in this last letter shows Frances at her best, revealing both broadmindedness, and kindness of heart. ' My cousin Murehead told me your Lordship wrot to him concerning some vacant stipents which are in me to dispose of; I desire they may be given to such poor ministers as have bine disposest of them, and to whom they did heeretofore belong, and in case that those individuall persons should be dead, then to such others as shall have bine put out of theyre liveings for no other faith but tenderness of consiance, and who has the greatest charge of poor inosent babes which perhaps are now starveing. I do confess I have great compassion for all such poor little creaturs, who have never yet offended God or man, therefore again,

[1] A yellow metal resembling brass.
[2] Lennoxlove Papers.
[3] Ibid March 19th, 169(9).

La Belle Stuart 245

My Lord, I must recommend this to you as that which I think a greater act of piety than even building of churches.'

For the remainder of her life the Duchess, now more or less an invalid, lived in peaceful retirement, from which she rarely emerged save for very exceptional occasions such as the Coronation of Queen Anne, which she attended on St. George's Day, April 23rd, 1702. Through the summer her health grew rapidly worse, and when the autumn came she knew that her end was near. On September the 24th she made her will, and only a few weeks later, on October the 15th, she died at the age of fifty four.

She was buried at her own desire close to where her husband had been laid nearly thirty years before in the Richmond vault, which occupies one of the small chapels that form the apse of Henry VII's. chapel in Westminster Abbey. The hideous monument which stands over her last resting-place was already there during her lifetime, having originally been erected to the memory of her husband's great-uncle Ludovic Stuart, Duke of Richmond and Lennox,[1] cousin of James I., by his widow, another Frances. It would have been a singularly inappropriate memorial to erect to Frances herself.

Four enormous female figures representing Faith,

---

[1] Since Ludovic had no son his title of Richmond expired with him. His brother Esmé succeeded to the Duchy of Lennox. The title of Duke of Richmond was again conferred by Charles I. on Esmé's son James, 4th Duke of Lennox, in 1641.

Hope, Prudence, and Charity support a vast gilded dome resembling a bird-cage ; this again is surmounted by an ungainly figure of Fame blowing a golden trumpet. These figures with their over-generous proportions and legs of exceptional muscular development now mark the last resting-place of the fair fragile lady whose gracefulness was one of her chief charms, and who ever took the utmost pride in the slenderness and exquisite formation of her nether limbs. It was appositely if not truly reported of her that an ambassador, on arriving in England and calling on her, begged her as a favour to let him see almost up to her knee, so as to be able to write to his master to confirm what he had heard about the perfection of her calf and ankle.[1]

By her express desire a waxen effigy of herself was set up near the tomb. " It is my will to have my Effigie as well done in wax as can bee and set up neare the old Duke Lodowick and Dutchesse Frances of Richmond and Lenox, put in a presse by itself distinct from the other with cleare crowne glasse before it and dressed in my Coronation robes and coronett."[2] Such effigies had long formed an

[1] C.A. 137. f. 400. This allusion was evidently meant for Frances, though it actually refers to Mary Villiers, Duchess of Richmond, widow of Duke James. The paper from which it is taken is a budget of piquant and probably more or less apocryphal anecdotes of personages at the English Court. The writer has inextricably entangled the personalities and careers of the two Duchesses of Richmond.

[2] The Duchess of Richmond's Will.

La Belle Stuart 247

indispensable part of the funeral regalia at the obsequies of great personages, and were rather costly. In one of the executors' accounts[1] of the Duchess's estate (June 1703) is an entry relating to this one : ' To Mr. Goldsmith for the performing of her Grace's Effigies, Glass, Jappanning, Bringing home, and setting up in K. Kenry 7th Chappell £260.' The taste of a later age condemned these waxworks as unfit ornaments for a Church, and such of them as had survived were removed in 1830 to another part of the Abbey. In an inexpressibly dreary loft the Duchess now stands in company with the waxen dummies of other illustrious dead. Nothing could be more sordid and depressing than this grotesque array of corpse-like figures in their dingy and bedraggled finery. There are eleven of them all told, a queerly assorted crew, most of them contemporaries of the Duchess of Richmond. Here is her old admirer, Charles II., a rakish figure with a cravat of real point-lace and a sardonic grin ; here also are three other sovereigns of her time, William of Orange, and his consort Mary II., and Queen Anne. George Monk, the great Duke of Albemarle, is there in battered armour, and a Duchess of Buckingham with her two sons. She was the last wife of that very Lord Mulgrave, who earlier in his career had been one of Frances Stuart's suitors. He was created

[1] Lennoxlove Papers.

a Duke by Queen Anne. But the effigies are not all of Stuart times; in glaring incongruity to these stand three other figures, the great Chatham, Horatio, Viscount Nelson, and Good Queen Bess! The effigy of Frances, which is one of the most revolting, is clad in the dress which she had worn at the Coronation of Queen Anne, a brocaded skirt with a bodice and train of crimson velvet. Where jewels once sparkled on her breast, there now cling only a few fragments of discoloured glass. In one hand she carries an artificial rose, in the other a fan. A pathetic interest attaches to the little stuffed green parrot with a red tail, which sits on a perch by her side. The story runs that it lived with her for forty years or more and died of grief a few days after her death. If this be true, she must have brought it over with her from France when she first came as a young girl to the Court of Charles II.

Considering that most of the Duchess's sources of income were in the nature of life-interests, which came to an end with her death, the fortune she was able to leave behind her in money and personal effects was fairly large. Such a result can only have been achieved by careful management, avoidance of wanton extravagance, and judicious expenditure on things worth while. It was not the effect of miserliness; for Frances had never been mean either to herself or to others. She had never stinted herself, had never, for instance, attempted to restrain her passion for dress, on which throughout her life she had spent considerable sums.[1] Nor had she thought only of herself, for she was generous to her friends and servants, and charitable to the poor and unfortunate. But the money she spent was well spent and not frittered away on useless trifles, as was proved by the considerable sums obtained at the sale after her death of her jewels and her collection of pictures and drawings. She had always refrained from spending money which she did not possess, and had scrupulously avoided running into debt. The fact that at the time of her death she owed only £101 14s. 1d.,[2] consisting for the most part of tradesmen's current accounts for her household expenses, shows the manner of her living. By such means she had succeeded in building up a small fortune, which she could dispose of as she wished. Such annuities as she received from the Crown together with her life-interest in the Lennox estates came to an end with her life. This was, of course, only right, but it was rather unjust that her heirs were obliged to surrender to the Crown her residence

---

[1] There has survived a bill due to 'Agnes Curson at ye Squirrel in Duke Street near Lincolns inn fields.' It was for holland and cambric for 'nightsmocks, daysmocks, and petticoats,' and amounted to £79.17.4½. Unlike most of the Duke's bills, it was paid in full. Egerton MSS. 2435. f.35.

An entry in the Treasury Books shows that the Duchess was occasionally in the habit of procuring clothes from France. Treasury Books VIII. (Oct. 5. 1686).

[2] Lennoxlove Papers.

in the Privy Garden at Whitehall, without any compensation for the considerable sums of money expended by the late Duke and Duchess on rebuilding and improvements.[1]

The manner in which she disposed of her property reveals the same qualities that she had shown in her letters. Her pride in her birth, her love for her family and friends, her generosity, her pity for the unfortunate, and above all her levelheadedness and common sense, all these, her most distinguished characteristics, are observable. There is a persistent legend that she left annuities to certain female friends with the burden of maintaining her cats, and this circumstance is supposed to have occasioned Pope's famous lines. 'Money,' says the Poet, ' cannot purchase either a friend or an heir '—

> "But thousands die without or this or that
> Die, and endow a college or a cat."[2]

It is perhaps sufficient to say that the word ' cat ' is not mentioned in the Duchess's will in any connection whatsoever. Frances was not the sort of woman to attach such conditions to an annuity. On the other hand she was just the sort of woman to

---

[1] Lennoxlove Papers. Memorial of Lord Blantyre to the Lords Commissioners of the Treasury.

[2] Pope's Moral Essays Epistle III.

keep a cat, even more than one cat, and the fact that some of the ladies who benefited by her will, may have taken it upon themselves to provide a home for her orphaned pets, possibly gave rise to the misleading story.

Several ladies did actually receive minor legacies, as did all her servants, amongst some of whom her wardrobe was also to be divided. There were charitable bequests to various old people, to ' my little poore monthly pensioners,' and to the poor of the Parish of St. Margaret's, Westminster. To her mother she left a legacy of £500 and £300 a year for life. The old lady lived to receive only the first instalment, dying a few months after her daughter.[1] The Duchess's cousin and namesake Frances Stuart, daughter of Lord Blantyre, also received a small legacy.

Frances's sister Sophia, Lady Bulkeley, was a Jacobite, living in France with the exiled Court at St. Germains. The Duchess states in her will that she would have wished to leave her a legacy of £1000 and £500 to each of her two sons and four daughters,[2] but is advised that she cannot do so owing to their estrangement from the existing government. She therefore makes provision that

---

[1] Her will is at Somerset House.

[2] One of these daughters married the famous Marshal of France, James Fitzjames, Duke of Berwick, son of James II. by Arabella Churchill.

to such of them as should return to England within seven years and 'be taken into the favour and protection of the Crown and discharged and freed from the offences against the same,' the bequests are to take effect.

But these are merely minor bequests. The bulk of the property was to be applied to a purpose that is most characteristic of the Duchess.

Plate, jewels, goods and chattels, everything in fact that she possessed, save what was otherwise disposed of in her will, was to be realized by her executors, Lawrence, Earl of Rochester, Alexander, Lord Blantyre, Sir William Whitelocke Kt., and and James Gray Esqre. After the minor legacies were paid and her debts discharged, the residue was to be invested in a purchase of lands in the kingdom of Scotland, 'which estate when purchased shall be called and I appoint the same to be named and called Lennoxlove.' It was to be settled on Walter Stuart, Master of Blantyre, and his heirs male. The young man to be made worthy of his high position was to be 'educated according to his quality and sent to travell for 2 or 3 yeares at the least for his improvement.' Lennoxlove was to be preserved 'in the heires male of that family soe long as the same can be done by the Lawes of that kingdom in perpetuall remembrance of mee."

In accordance with her desire a great part of her property was realized. Certain of the more important pictures were already left to friends, amongst them several to the late Duke's sister, Lady Catherine O'Brien, which shows that the reconciliation between the two ladies had endured. Full-length pictures of herself and of her husband were left to Lord Blantyre 'to be preserved in the family and by virtue of an old promise I made to him long since.' The rest of her pictures and drawings, including works by Leonardo da Vinci, Raphael, Paolo Veronese, Oliver, Hilliard, and Cooper were dispersed by auction at her lodgings in Whitehall shortly after her death.[1] Her china, plate and household goods were also sold, and in the spring of the next year her jewels were disposed of "in the Apollo Chamber adjoyning to the Old Devil Tavern by Temple Bar," fetching £3937 1s., exclusive of her pearl necklace, appraised at £1200, which did not immediately find a buyer.[2]

With the money thus obtained, nearly £10,000, a considerable sum in those days,[3] land was purchased in East Lothian, Dumbartonshire, Renfrewshire, and Berwickshire. The East Lothian estate, bought from Lord Teviott, was the historic Lethington, with its famous old castle, which had been in the possession of the Maitland family for several centuries and was the home of the celebrated William Maitland of Lethington, Secretary of State to Mary, Queen of

[1] London Gazette No. 3862. November 1702.
[2] Lennoxlove Papers.
[3] Ibid. James Gray's Account. June 1st, 1703.

Scots. This property was the one chosen to receive the name of Lennoxlove in accordance with the instructions of the Duchess.

Though Walter Stuart lived long enough not only to receive Lennoxlove, but also to succeed his father as Lord Blantyre in 1704, he had but few years in which to enjoy his inheritance. He died of fever in 1713, and was buried near the Duchess in Westminster Abbey. As he had died unmarried he was succeeded by his younger brother Robert. Lennoxlove actually was 'preserved in the heires male of that family,' till the death of the 12th and last Lord Blantyre in 1900. But since Lord Blantyre was succeeded by a grandson, the connection by blood remains unbroken to this day.

Lennoxlove is Frances Stuart's real monument. Truly it can be said that the estate has been held ' in perpetuall remembrance ' of her. Her wishes have been followed in the spirit as well as in the letter, and she is held, as she would have desired to be held, the presiding deity of the place. The portraits she gave to Lord Blantyre still hang in places of honour. Appropriately enough in the Lennoxlove portrait she is not the lovely gay Frances Stuart of her girlhood, but the majestic Duchess of Richmond and Lennox, with stately robes and ermine-lined cloak befitting her exalted rank, and at her side a velvet cushion bearing a ducal coronet. The Duke's portrait also shows him at his stateliest

FRANCES TERESA STUART, DUCHESS OF RICHMOND
AND LENNOX
W. Wissing and J. Van der Vaart

in Garter Robes[1] with white wand of office, and in the background an anchor, the symbol of his exalted position as Lord High Admiral of Scotland. Nor are these the only objects at Lennoxlove that bring the Duchess to the memory. There also is the superb silver-gilt toilet-service of French workmanship, given to her by Charles the Second. It was obviously presented to her after her marriage, as it bears a ducal coronet and her monogram as Duchess of Richmond. A tortoise-shell cabinet adorned with the Royal Arms is reputed also to have been a gift from His Majesty. There too is a lacquer chest which she is said to have used as her jewel-box. But perhaps one of the most interesting objects of all is her watch. One cannot help feeling that this belonged to ' La Belle Stuart ' rather than to the Duchess of Richmond and Lennox. Made by Isaac Pluvier, a Dutch clock-maker, who settled in London in 1641 and died there in 1665, it is of exquisite design and workmanship. On the face is enamelled a curious picture. At the foot of a tree in a flowery meadow a naked lady lies on a couch strewn with blossoms. Above her flies the little God of Love about to let fly an arrow from his bow. In the distance can be discerned approaching a gay cavalier in the costume of Charles II's. time. He is evidently to be the recipient of those favours which Cupid's

[1] The Duke's Garter Robes are still preserved at Lennoxlove.

arrow will induce the lady to grant. A very gallant watch, and one which would have appealed immensely to the whimsical humour of the King! Whether the artist possessed a subtle sense of humour or merely a perverted sense of direction is not now to be decided, but at all events it is clear that Cupid's aim is so erratic that his arrow could not possibly transfix the recumbent nymph! Intentionally or not it epitomizes Frances Stuart's career.

It was Frances Stuart's beauty that made her famous in her own day; her mind and character have always seemed of much less importance than her appearance, which explains why posterity has for the most part been content to accept Gramont's unfavourable estimate of her, without troubling to question its justice. The Chevalier, though lavish in his tributes to her surpassing beauty, is inclined to be ungenerous, even unjust, in his opinion of her other qualities. She was beautiful, but she was a fool! That is the impression of her he intended to convey. But if she be judged by the evidence afforded by her own career, by the opinions which others than Gramont expressed of her, will not a somewhat different impression arise? It is possible that Gramont, judging her as she seemed to be, in those years of careless gaiety at the beginning of the reign, was genuinely deceived as to her true character. To him, as to many others, she appeared to be entirely frivolous, regardless of everything else in the world but her own pleasure, vain of her beauty, and continually demanding to be admired and spoilt. What he did not realize was that this was only her manner; her carelessness was all on the surface; in reality she was cool and level-headed, possessed of very definite principles from which she was firmly determined neither to be forced nor persuaded. How else than by acute common sense and great strength of will could she have kept her virtue inviolate in one of the most immoral Courts in Europe? That she did succeed in doing so seems now to be incontestable.

Prudence, common sense, and self-control had enabled her to overcome all her difficulties. Her character was not subtle or brilliant, it was merely steadfast. Though her heart was naturally disposed to generosity and affection, she had never let it run away with her. Coolly and collectedly, almost callously, she would think everything out, and, when she had once made up her mind, nothing would induce her to change it. There was often perhaps too much obstinacy in her firmness when she felt that she was in the right. Scottish caution made her slow in forming a belief, but once it was definitely formed it remained as immovable as a rock.

Her mental endowments were adequate though not brilliant. She had a good business head, and was perfectly capable of managing her own financial affairs, and, if necessary, other people's, to the best advantage. She was not witty, but she possessed a happy and graceful way of expressing herself—which is the next best thing, for charm will often cover an absence of wit. She was pre-eminently a woman of taste. The best-dressed woman of her time, she did not neglect other forms of art. She displayed some interest in literature, and especially in the theatre, though Lee may have been exaggerating a little when he expatiated on her 'extraordinary love for heroick poetry.' She was extremely fond of music, and was generally considered the best dancer at the English Court. Her own collection of pictures was well-chosen, while she contributed as much as possible to the art of her own day by having her beauty perpetuated by almost every portrait-painter at Court.

From her extraordinary care for her good name, a surprising trait in anyone of Charles II's. Court, it may be concluded that La Belle Stuart rated virtue as only second to beauty. Yet it is doubtful whether her passionate chastity was due so much to high ideas of the essential worth of morality as to a purely aesthetic revulsion from the actualities of physical love. For, although she shrank from the facts of love and passion was abhorrent to her, by her undisguised pleasure in men's admiration for her and her fondness for romantic dalliance, she herself increased the danger to be apprehended from those who would have wished to conquer her resistance. She was as one who loved to linger in the outskirts of a forest, but would not venture to plunge into its heart.

Hers was a temperament which would have puzzled this age less than her own. She was not understood by the Court of Charles II. Yet she never intended to deceive anyone as to her true character. That childish frivolity of hers was not a mask; it was just the butterfly gaiety of spoilt youth, and, as she grew older, it disappeared. Of her it may truly be said that she knew how and when to grow up. Her character deepened and expanded in just the same way that the wild-rose loveliness of her girlhood gradually changed into the stately beauty of her later years. But it is for her beauty that she always has been and always will be remembered. There is nothing less evanescent than Beauty, it dies only when it is forgotten.

APPENDIX

THE PORTRAITS OF LA BELLE STUART

An attempt to discover all the portraits of a person who died over two hundred years ago is for obvious reasons a difficult and thankless task. Although those which are in well-known collections are easily to be found in books of reference, there are always more to which public attention has never been drawn. A further complication is added by a regrettable tendency to christen unidentified portraits capriciously with the names of illustrious statesmen and soldiers, famous writers, and reigning beauties. Many a nameless portrait of a lady of Charles II's. time is on no sufficient grounds supposed to represent Nell Gwynne, Lady Castlemaine, the Duchess of Portsmouth, or La Belle Stuart ! This arbitrary method of naming portraits has of recent years produced a natural reaction, and the present tendency is to go to the other extreme and question the identification of even the best-known portraits.

It is almost impossible to reconcile with one another all the portraits of the Duchess of Richmond. In his endeavour to determine which are the authentic portraits the present writer has been influenced by two considerations—pedigree and resemblance. This

La Belle Stuart 261

latter ground is less reliable than would be expected, especially in the case of pictures of this very mannered period, and it is risky to reject any portrait of established reputation, even when it bears little resemblance to the others.

Although the writer has naturally been concerned more with the subject than with the painters of these pictures, wherever possible he has endeavoured to identify the painter also. Most portraits of this period are confidently attributed to Lely, but in the case of some of these pictures it has been found possible to suggest a more likely begetter.

The best-known portrait of Frances Stuart, the picture of her as Diana among the Lely 'Beauties' at Hampton Court, has recently been challenged; but its history appears to be sufficiently well established to dispose of all doubts. From the Catalogue of King James II's. pictures it is certain that the Duchess of Richmond is among the Lely 'Beauties,' and, according to Mr. Ernest Law, all the others are satisfactorily accounted for. This particular picture was certainly considered to be 'La Belle Stuart' as early as 1713, a decade after the Duchess's death; for in that year George Vertue, the engraver, mentions among the Windsor[1] ' Beauties ' : ' Dutches Richmond *with a bow in her left hand.*'[2] This picture has been engraved several times; by Thomas

[1] The Lely 'Beauties,' now at Hampton Court Palace, were formerly at Windsor Castle.
[2] Add MSS. 23,068

Watson, 1779; E. Scriven, 1810; J. Thomson, 1819; and S. Freeman, 1827. The portrait in the collection of the Duke of Buccleuch and Queensberry at Dalkeith House appears to be a repetition of this picture.

The authenticity of the portrait in His Majesty's collection at Buckingham Palace is incontrovertible. The picture was seen by Pepys in Jacob Huysman's house on August 26th, 1664 : " Mrs. Stewart in a buff doublet like a soldier." In James II's. Catalogue it is mentioned as : ' No. 465. By Housman, Dutchess of Richmond in man's apparel, half-length.' It has been engraved as a frontispiece for the ' Iconographia Scotica,' " Johnson del, Rivers sculp., 1796."

Equally beyond doubt is the full-length portrait at Lennoxlove bequeathed by the Duchess to Alexander, Lord Blantyre, together with the Lely portrait of her husband. It was painted by William Wissing, assisted by Jan Van der Vaart, who, though himself a painter of respectable gifts, occasionally contented himself with painting draperies for Wissing. The picture is dated 1687, and therefore represents the Duchess at the age of 39. She is dressed in a brown robe fastened with diamond clasps and wears a blue cloak edged and lined with miniver and adorned with a band of gold and pearl embroidery. There is a mezzotint of this picture ; head and shoulders only, in an oval, " W. Wissing pinxit. R. Williams fecit."

La Belle Stuart

The other portrait in Major Baird's collection reputed to be Frances Stuart almost undoubtedly represents Mary Villiers, Duchess of Richmond. It was, however, sold at the Stowe Sale in 1848 as Frances Stuart.

There are four portraits in the collection of the Duke of Richmond at Goodwood. The full-length of Frances Stuart as Pallas is attributed to Lely in the Goodwood Catalogue, and to Huysman in the catalogue of the Exhibition of the Royal House of Stuart, 1889. The true painter is probably Gascar. This painter was in the habit of engraving mezzotints after his own pictures and is likely to have been the engraver of a very rare mezzotint of this picture inscribed ' H. Gascar pinx. Frances Theresa, Duchess of Richmont.' The fact that the picture is ascribed to Gascar on a contemporary mezzotint should be regarded as evidence of great weight. Both Mr. J. D. Milner and Mr. C. H. Collins Baker consider the style of this painting to be typical of Gascar. In the later engravings published by Messrs. Harding and Lepard it is described as a Lely. All these show the picture at ¾ length only : Drawn by Wm. Derby, Engraved by J. Thomson, 1823 ; Engraved by J. Thomson, 1827 ; Engraved by H. T. Ryall, 1830. Another full-length at Goodwood shows the Duchess in a black dress with a red robe jewelled all round the border. Her arm rests on a stone pedestal carved with amorini. The early and rare mezzotint of this is inscribed : ' P. Lely Eques pinxit. Sold by Alex Browne at ye blew balcony in little Queen Street.' In a fascinating half-length the Duchess is wearing a blue dress with a red mantle over the right shoulder and a veil falling from the back of her head. The mezzotint of this is inscribed : ' P. Lelly Eques pinxit. Beckett fecit. E. Cooper exc.' The fourth portrait at Goodwood is also ascribed to Lely. The Duchess is shown at ¾ length in a yellow robe over a white underdress and a blue mantle fastened with jewels on the left shoulder. There does not appear to be an engraving of this picture.

A well-known picture is that in the collection of Viscount Cobham at Hagley Hall. It has at various times been ascribed to Lely, Greenhill, and Riley, but is now pretty well acknowledged to be by Huysman. It has been suggested that this picture really represents Mary, Duchess of Buckingham, and this seems not unlikely, for it bears little resemblance to any other portrait of the Duchess of Richmond, and none to the picture by Huysman at Buckingham Palace. It was, however, engraved as the Duchess of Richmond for Harding's edition of the Gramont memoirs. ' Miss Stewart, afterwards Duchess of Richmond. From an original picture by Sir Peter Lely in the collection of Lord Westcote at Hagley Park. S. Harding del. W. N. Gardiner, sculp.' In the absence therefore of more definite evidence to the contrary this picture must still be numbered among the portraits of the Duchess of Richmond.

To Mr. J. D. Milner is due the identification as La Belle Stuart of the picture in Earl Spencer's collection at Althorp formerly called 'Anne Hyde, Duchess of York.' The resemblance to other portraits of Frances Stuart is marked, while there is little likeness to Anne Hyde, who was never so handsome. The Duchess is here dressed in brown with a drapery of brown brocade of a deeper tone.

The picture now known as 'La Belle Stuart' in Lord Sackville's collection at Knole is negligible both as a likeness of the lady and as a work of art. In the same room, on the other hand, is an undoubted portrait of the Duchess as a saint with a palm-branch in her hand. This picture is No. 140 in the Knole Catalogue, 'Portrait of a lady. Half-length.'

Two more full-lengths of the Duchess are known, one at Castle Howard, and the other in the possession of Mr. H. O. Goodwin. The latter picture, in which the Duchess wears a helmet and carries a spear, formerly belonged to the Vernon family.

A portrait called 'The Duchess of Richmond, by Sir Peter Lely' at the Great Eastern Railway Hotel at Liverpool Street appears to the writer to be one of those arbitrarily named. Although a contemporary portrait of some merit it certainly does not represent the Duchess of Richmond, nor is the style of painting anything like Lely's.

Many portraits or alleged portraits of Frances

Stuart have come into the market during the last two hundred years, but it will readily be understood that it has been impossible to trace their present whereabouts. In spite of Messrs. Christie's courteous assistance the writer has been unable to find the present owner of the portrait sold on June 3rd, 1893. This picture by Largillière represented the Duchess at the age of forty, wearing a large three-cornered hat and holding a King Charles spaniel. It has also been impossible to trace the Lely portrait from the Townshend collection, sold at Christie's in 1904. The Duchess, dressed as St. Agnes in a white dress with blue drapery, bears a palm-branch in one hand and caresses a lamb with the other.

Portraits attributed to Lely were sold by Cock in 1724 and by Christie's in 1835, 1838 and 1863. The last that came into the market was a Lely portrait belonging to the Duke of Fife. This was sold in 1907 and subsequently went to America.

Other portraits which have gone into obscurity are a Lely which was sold at the Strawberry Hill Sale in 1842 and a portrait of the Duchess dressed in white silk. In the middle of the last century this picture was in the possession of the Rev. J. E. Waldy. Pictures which disappeared still earlier into obscurity are a drawing, which, according to Horace Walpole,[1] was made by one Henry Anderton,

[1] Anecdotes of Painting.

and a full-length portrait mentioned in an inventory of the goods in Dublin Castle belonging to the Duke of Ormonde in 1678. This is no longer in the possession of the Duke's descendants and probably disappeared when the last Duke of Ormonde was attainted in 1715. It is to be hoped that these notes will have the effect of bringing some at least of these lost pictures to light.

In addition to the paintings there is a well-known and interesting mezzotint, designed and executed by R. Robinson. In it the Duchess is arrayed in all the flamboyant panoply of a coronation dress, most elaborately broidered, befurred, and bejewelled.

One more mezzotint should be mentioned, because, although it is a poor production, it is often to be met with. It is inscribed: ' P. Lely pinxt. C. Turner sculpt. Frances Stuart, Duchess of Richmond from an original painting by Sir Peter Lely, ob 1702, London. Published by S. Woodburn, 1810.' The writer has not discovered the original of which this is the engraving.

MINIATURES

Samuel Cooper painted several miniatures of Frances Stuart. The best-known is a fine work in His Majesty's collection at Windsor Castle. This is the portrait which Pepys mentioned as ' now just done before her having the small pox.' It is one of a series of five specially executed for Charles II. All are unfinished except for the heads. They represent Catherine of Bragança, the Duchess of Richmond, Lady Castlemaine, the Duke of Monmouth, and George Monk, Duke of Albemarle. There is a smaller replica of this miniature of Frances Stuart in the collection of the Duke of Beaufort.

Three other miniatures by Cooper are also at Windsor Castle, and, like the first, have remained in the royal collection ever since they were painted. (Nos. 1164, 1165, and 1166 in James II's. Catalogue). One of these portrays the Duchess standing at ¾ length, dressed as a page in periwig and richly-laced red coat. Her fondness for dressing as a man is also exemplified in the miniature by Cooper at the Rijks Museum, Amsterdam. She is wearing a black hat with white plumes and a grey dress with black collar. Her lace cravat is tied with a blue ribbon. This miniature was formerly in the Royal Collection at the Mauritshuis at the Hague, and prior to that was in the possession of the Princes of Orange.

A miniature in the collection of the Duke of Buccleuch and Queensberry, signed S. Cooper and dated 1654, appears to be an early 19th century adaptation of the Hampton Court portrait.

MEDALS

Besides the medals representing Frances Stuart as Britannia there are two portrait-medals also by Jan Roettier. The smaller of these is wrought on a thin sheet of gold, and was probably intended to be worn in a locket.

INDEX

A

Aberdeen, Earl of, 229
Absolom and Achitophel,' 44
Additional MSS., referred to, 132, 134, 136-9, 154 note, 165-6, 168, 170-4, 178-9, 180-2, 192-3, 195-201, 207-210, 212, 214, 261
Albemarle, Duke of, 85, 164, 247, 268
Althorp, portrait of Frances Stuart at, 265
Anderton, Henry, drawing of Frances Stuart by, 266
Anne, Queen, 241, 245, 247
Annesley, Lord, 214
Apollo Chamber, 253
Argencourt, Mlle. de La Motte, 58
Arlington, Lord, 53, 83, 90, 118, 129, 165-6, 169, 170, 172, 174, 186, 188-9, 194, see also Bennet, Sir Henry
Ashley, Lord, 87, 168, 169, 170, 171, 181, 207
Aubigny, almoner to the Queen, 13
Aubigny, George, Lord, father of the Duke of Richmond, 102
Aubigny, dukedom of, 147-8, 165, 221

B

Bath, John Granville, Earl of, 166-7, 169, 170, 171, 240
Bath, Marquess of, letters in collection of, referred to, 149, 213
Batten, Sir William, 121
'Bear at the Bridgefoot,' 113
Beaufort, MSS., referred to, 15
Beaufort, Duke of, miniature of Frances Stuart in collection of, 262

Bennet, Sir Henry, 48, 53, 61, see also Arlington, Lord
Berkeley, 40, see also Fitzhardinge, Lord
Berkley, Lord, 125, 126
Berkshire House, 152
Berwick, James Fitzjames, Duke of 251, note
Bickerstaff, Sir Charles, 217
Bigorre, secretary to the French Embassy, 85
Black Dick, 172 and note
Blantyre, 1st Lord, 64
Blantyre, 4th Lord, 3
Blantyre, 5th Lord, 228 et seq, 233 et seq., 238, 240, 242, 252, 253, 262
Blantyre, Lady, 244
Blantyre, 12th and last Lord, 254
Bombay, 8
Boreman, J., 134-5
Bowling-green at Whitehall, 112, 158, 159
Boynton, Mrs. 15
Breda, 136, 141, 148
Bristol, Earl of, 9, 168, 173, 179
Brouncker, Lord, 94, 197
Buccleuch MSS., referred to, 15
Buccleuch and Queensberry, Duke of, picture of Frances Stuart in collection of, 262
Buccleuch and Queensberry, Duke of, miniature of Frances Stuart in collection of, 268
Buckhurst, Lord, 214
Buckingham, George Villiers, Duke of, 43-48, 50-53, 61, 119, 123, 129, 203, 237
Buckingham, Mary Fairfax, Duchess of, wife of the preceding, 47, 48, 182-185, 264
Buckingham, John Sheffield, Duke of, his 'Works' referred to, 28, 162, see also Lord Mulgrave

INDEX

Buckingham Palace, 76, 262
Bulkely, Henry, husband of Sophia Stuart, 159
Bulkely, Sophia, see Stuart, Sophia
Burnet, Bishop, his 'History of His Own Time,' referred to, 100, 112, 121, 123, 124, 130, note, 186
'Butterfly,' 49, 50

C

Calash, Story of the, 73
Calendar of State Papers, Domestic, referred to 90, 112, 158, 211
Calendar of State Papers. Foreign. Denmark, referred to 193-5, 197, 205-6, 209, 213
Calendar of State Papers, Scotland, referred to 211
Campden, Viscountess, 221 note
Canterbury, Archbishop of, 85, 123
Capel, Sir Henry, 218
Carlingford, Lord, 56
Carlos II, King of Spain, 135
Cary, Mrs, 15
Castle Howard, 265
Castlemaine, Barbara Villiers, Countess of, 16 et seq, 25, 26, 33, 35, 37-41, 51, 59, 64, 65, 69, 71-74, 79, 80, 82, 83, 86, 90, 91, 94, 97, 99, 100, 107, 108, 118, 123, 124, 129, 131, 144, 152, 155, 158, 176, 260, 268
Castlemaine, Roger Palmer, Earl of, 17
Catherine of Bragança, Queen of Charles II, 8, 9, 11-15, 18-22, 24, 40-42, 51, 52, 62, 63, 66, 71, 73, 84, 90, 95, 99, 110 et seq, 157, 158, 177, 182-186, 226
Cavendish, Elizabeth, first wife of the Duke of Richmond, 103
Chaillot, Convent of, 4
Chancellor, Lord, see Clarendon
Charles I, 49
Charles II, restoration of, 1; early struggles, 5; marriage projected, 7-8; letter to

Charles II (*continued*)
Madam quoted, 9; marriage of, 13-15; appoints Lady Castlemaine Lady of the Bedchamber, 16; his quarrel with the Queen, 18 et seq; his entry into London, 24; enamoured of Frances Stuart, 27; his dislike for gambling, 28; receives Russian ambassadors, 31; Louis XIV's opinion of, 32; letter to Madame quoted, 37; quarrels with Lady Castlemaine, 39; riding with the Queen, 41; at Buckingham's party, 50-52; his hopes of an heir frustrated, 55; at Oxford, 59; his pursuit of Frances, 60-61; his distress at the Queen's illness, 63; his reply to Lady Castlemaine's relations 65; letter to Madame quoted, 66; takes to a periwig, 68; his divided love, 69; letter to Madame quoted, 72; his designs on Frances Jennings abandoned, 73; visits Portsmouth, 84; his dislike for Salisbury, 85; goes for a progress in Dorset, 88; meets Parliament at Oxford, ibid; his strained relations with his brother, 89; letter to Madame quoted, 90; his courage during the Great Fire, 97; adopts a new fashion, 98; his attitude towards the Richmond marriage 106 et seq; discovers Frances with Richmond, 108; pretends to countenance the marriage, 112; his rage at the elopement, 114; his dislike for Clarendon, 117 et seq; determines to dismiss him, 124; he suspects Lord Cornbury, ibid; burns Clarendon's letter to him, 128; refuses to forgive Frances, 133; rejects Madame's overtures, 146 et seq; letter to Madame quoted, 146; refuses to see Frances, 150; letter to Madame quoted, 151;

INDEX

Charles II (*continued*)
reconciled with Frances, 152; letters to Madame quoted, 153-4; his unconventional visit to Frances, 155-7; letters to Madame quoted, 157, 164; at Newmarket, 164; refuses to send Richmond to Poland, 172; no longer in love with Frances, 173; meets Madame off Dover, 177; attracted by Louise de Keroualle, ibid; at a masked ball, 184; boasts when drunk of his success with Frances, 186; at Euston, ibid; mock-marriage with Louise de Keroualle, 181; appoints Richmond ambassador to Denmark, ibid; a good friend to the widowed Duchess, 207; Richmond and Lennox titles and estates revert to, 208; his interview with James Percy, 220; his decision in the affairs of Jack How, 224; an expert dancer, 225; last illness of 231, ;death, 232
Charles VII, King of France, 147
Chesterfield, Earl and Countess of, 31, 32
Christie's, 266
Clarendon, Edward Hyde, Earl of, 7, 13, 16, 20 *et seq*, 38, 48, 89, 90, 91, 117-130
Clarendon, Earl of, his 'Continuation' to his 'Life' referred to, 22, 92, 125, 130 note
Clarendon and Rochester Correspondence, 240
Clarendon House, 122
Claudius, the Roman Emperor, 142
Cleveland, Duchess of, 222, see also Castlemaine, Countess of
Clinkard, 201
Cobham Hall, Kent, 103, 104, 110, 113, 116, 133-135, 137, 145, 148, 149, 159, 178, 180, 198, 208, 216, 217, 219
Cobham, Viscount, picture of Frances Stuart in collection of 264
Cock, 266

Colbert de Croissy, French Ambassador, his despatches referred to, 168, 173, 184, 188-190, 192
Collins Baker, Mr C. H., 263
Colombes, Chateau, de, 4, 171
Comet of 1664, 76
Cominges, Comte de, French Ambassador, 32, his despatches referred to, 33, 38, 39, 40, 52, 55, 59, 60, 64, 65, 77
Cooper, E., engraving of Frances Stuart by, 264
Cooper, Samuel, miniature-painter, 154, 253, 267, 268
Copenhagen, 192, 193, 197
Cornbury, Lord, son of Clarendon 15, 124, 140, 210, 240
'Covent Garden Drollery,' referred to, 202 note
Coventry, Henry, 136, 140, 148-9, 195, 208, 213
Coventry, Sir John, 142, 149
Coventry, Sir William, 90, 129
Courtin, Honoré de, French Ambassador, 78, his despatches referred to, 79, 80-83, 86, 87, 140, 148, 225
Craven, Lord, 85
Crofts, William, Lord, 11
Cromwell, 5, 47
Croy, Madame le, palmist, 189
Curson, Agnes, 249 note

D

Dartmouth, Lord, his notes to Burnet referred to, 123, 186
D'Aulnoy, Comtesse, see **Dunois**
Davis, John, 90
Deal, 179
Denham, Lady, 83
Denmark, King of, 212, 213
Denton, Dr William, 113 note
'Depositions... relating to the Birth of the Prince of Wales, 239
Derby, Countess of, 225
Digby, Francis, 201, 202
Digby, Lord, 53
Dorset, 87, 103, 136, 140
Dorset Garden, 226

T

INDEX

Dover, 176-178
Dryden, John, 44, 163, 202, 203
Dunois, Countess, her 'Memoirs of the Court of England' referred to, 45, 49-50

E

Echard's History, referred to, 119, 130 note
Edgar, Saxon King, 144
Edgehill, Battle of, 16
Edinburgh, 134, 178
Effigy of Duchess of Richmond, 246-247
Egerton MSS, referred to, 177, 210, 249
Elmes, M, letter from, referred to, 153
Elsinore, 204-206
'Engagers,' 3
Enterkin, 242, 243,
Essex, Earl of, 179, 181, 197, 217-219, 224
Euston, 186, 187
Evelyn, John, diarist, 72, 85, 98, 114-116, 143, 153, 187

F

Fairfax, General, 46, 47
Fairfax, Mary, see Buckingham, Duchess of
Fane, Mr, 179
Falmouth, Earl of, 79
Falmouth, Countess of, 83
Farnham Castle, 84
Fell, Dr, Canon of Christ Church, 72
Fenton's edition of Waller's 'Works,' 145 note
Fife, Duke of, picture of Frances Stuart formerly in possession of, 266
Fitzharding, Lord, 70
Flexney, 139 and note, 198
Forneron's 'Louise de Keroualle' referred to, 76
Fraizer, Mrs, 15
'Francis,' the Duke of Richmond's yacht, 137

Freeman, Mr, 137
Freeman, S, engraving of Frances Stuart by, 262

G

Gardiner, W. N., engraving of Frances Stuart by, 264
Gascar, H, portrait of Frances Stuart by, 263
Gascoign, Sir Bernard, 182
Gerard, Lady, 176, 185
Goldsmith, Mr, 247
Goodwin, Mr H. O, portrait of Frances Stuart in possession of, 265
Goodwood House, pictures of Frances Stuart at, 263, 264
Gramont, Chevalier, de, 28, 55, 57, 58, 73, 105, 237, 256
Gramont Memoirs referred to, 26-32, 48, 52, 54-59, 73-74, 95, and note, 100, 105, 130 note, 214
Grandison, Lord, father of Lady Castlemaine, 16
Gravesend, 179, 214
Gray, James, 243, 252, 253 note
Green stockings, story of the, 31
Greenwich, 23, 75
'Guardinfantas,' 14
Guildford, Countess of, 147
Gwynne, Nell, 76, 95, 173, 260

H

Halifax, Lord, 224
Hamilton, Anthony, writer of the Gramont Memoirs, 56, 95 note
Hamilton, Elizabeth, afterwards Comtesse de Gramont, 56, 83, 105
Hamilton, George, 55-59
Hampton Court Palace, 14, 15, 23, 75, 80, 84, 90, 96, 180, 182, 185, 261
Harwich, 131
Hatton, Christopher, 132
Hatton Correspondence, referred to, 132, 185

INDEX

Hawkins's Medallic Illustrations of British History referred to, 144, 145
Henshaw, Mr, 192-194, 197, 206, 207, 209, 212, 213
Henriette Anne, Duchess of Orleans, 'Madame,' 5, 6, 10, 11, 19, 37, 66, 72, 90, 130 note, 146, 147, 151, 153, 154, 164, 165, 174-177
Henrietta Maria, mother of Charles II, 4-6, 10, 23, 62, 78, 132, 147
Herbert, Charles, Lord, 49
Herbert, Lady, see Richmond, Mary Villiers, Duchess of
Heron-Allen, E., his 'Selsey Bill, Historic and Prehistoric' referred to, 142
Herrick, Robert, quoted, 36, 93
Holles, Lord, 136, 148
How, Jack, 223, 224
Huddelston, Father, 232
Hugh, 243
Huysman, Jacob, painter, portraits of Frances Stuart by, 75, 76, 262-264
Hyde, Anne, Duchess of York, see York, Duchess of
Hyde, Edward, see Clarendon
Hyde Park, 74, 94

I

Ingilby Papers, referred to, 184
'Intelligence, The,' referred to, 84, 88

J

James II, 238, 240, 241, see also York, James, Duke of
James II's Catalogue, referred to, 261, 262, 268
Jennings, Frances, 72-73
Jermyn, the younger, 26, 167, 168
Jonson, Captain, 137

K

Keroualle, Louise de, 144, 177, 184, 187, 189, 190, 221, see also Portsmouth, Duchess of
Killigrew, 56
King, Dr, 231
King's Warrant Books, referred to, 208, 211
Kingston, 45, 80
Knole, portrait of Frances Stuart at, 265

L

La Garde, Mrs, 15, 106
Lambeth Palace, 11 note, 85
Largilliere, N. le, portrait of Frances Stuart by, 266
Law, Mr Ernest, 261
Lee, Nathaniel, 226 et seq, 258
Le Fleming MSS., referred to, 112, 116, 213
Lely, Sir Peter, portraits of Frances Stuart by, 29, 76, 83, 261-266
Lennox, Esmé, Duke of, 102, 245 note
Lennoxlove, 252-255, 262
Lennoxlove Papers, referred to, 228-230, 233-236, 241-244, 247, 249, 250, 253
L'Estrade, Monsieur, French representative at Breda, 148
Lethington, 253, 254, see also Lennoxlove
Levingstane, Sir James, afterwards Earl of Newburgh, 102
Lewis, Margaret, second wife of the Duke of Richmond, 104
Lichfield, Charlotte, Countess of, 239
Lichfield, Earl of, first title of the Duke of Richmond, 102
Lisbon, 12
London, Bishop of, 13
London Bridge, 113
London Gazette, referred to, 215, 253
Lorraine, Chevalier, de, 6, 7
Louis XIV, 8, 10, 32, 38, 58, 77, 78, 88, 122, 135, 147, 148, 155, 164, 165, 174-177, 221

Luttrell Collection, 215
Lyttelton, Sir Charles, 131

M

'Madame,' see Henriette Anne, Duchess of Orleans
Maitland, William, of Lethington, 253
Manchester, Earl of, Lord Chamberlain, 173, 174
Mandeville, Lord, 114
Mapelsden, Jarvis, 180, 198, 199
Marshal, Lady, 176, 185, 239
Marvell, Andrew, satirist, 144
Mary, Princess, afterwards Queen Mary II, 225
Mauritshuis, 268
Mazarin, Cardinal, 5
Medals, 142 et seq
Medway, Dutch fleet in the, 136
Miller, 138
Milner, Mr J. D., 263, 265
Molina, Count de, Spanish Ambassador, 80, 82
Monk, see Albemarle, Duke of
Monmouth, Duchess of, 185, see also Scott, Lady Anne
Monmouth, James, Duke of, illegitimate son of Charles II, 37, 165, 177, 224, 225, 268
'Monsieur,' see Orleans, Duke of
Montagu, Edward, 61
Montagu, Ralph, English Ambassador in Paris, 174
'Mother of the Maids,' 210
Mountstevens, Mr, 223 note
Mulgrave, Lord, 162-164, 219-221 247, see also Buckingham, John Sheffield, Duke of
Muscovy, Tsar of, embassy from, 30
Muskerry, Lord and Lady, 95 note

N

Newburgh, Earl of, 103, see also Levingstane, Sir James
'Newes, The,' referred to, 84
Newmarket, 164, 181
Norfolk, 186

Northumberland, Joscelin Percy, Earl of, 220
Norwich, Earl of, 214
Norwich, 187

O

O'Brien, Lady Catherine, 200, 208, 216-218, 253, see also Stuart, Lady Catherine
O'Brien, Lord, 200 note, 219
Orange, Dowager Princess of, 7
Orange, Prince of, 184, 238, see also William III
Orleans, Duke of, Monsieur, 6, 7, 175, 176, 178
Orleans, Duchess of, see Henriette Anne
Ormonde, Duke of, 105
Ormonde, Duke of, picture of Frances Stuart formerly in possession of, 267
Oxford, 59, 88-90

P

Palmer, Mrs, see Castlemaine, Countess of
Palmer, Roger, see Castlemaine, Earl of
Paul, Sir John, 204-206
Payne, Roger, 139 and note, 198, 201
Pembroke, Lord, 85
Pepys, Samuel, diarist, 35, 41, 42, 61, 63, 65, 68-71, 75, 85, 89-91, 94, 96-102, 107, 112-116, 120, 121, 130 note, 143, 150-155, 158, 159, 197, 237, 262, 267
Percy, James, 220
Persian mode, 98
Peterborough, Lord, 12
Pett, the ship-builder, 196
Philip IV, King of Spain, 135
Pierce, 116
Plague, The Great, 79 et seq
Pluvier, Isaac, watchmaker, 255
'Poems on Affairs of State,' referred to, 144, 189, 222, 227, 239
Pope, Alexander, 250
Porter, 49, 50

INDEX

Portsmouth, Louise de Keroualle, Duchess of, 76, 177, 222, 225, 260, see also Keroualle
Portsmouth, 13, 14, 84
Portugal, Queen Regent of, 12, 70, 94
Portugal, Infanta, of, see Catherine of Bragança
Pregnani, the Abbé, 164, 165, 174
Price, Mrs, 15
Pudding Lane, 96

Q

Queen-Mother, see Henrietta Maria
Queroel, see Keroualle
Querouaille, see Keroualle

R

Ratten, Mr, 140
Raynham, 186
'Rehearsal, The,' 44, 203
Richmond in Surrey, 39, 40, 82
Richmond and Gordon, Duke of, pictures of Frances Stuart in collection of, 263, 264
Richmond and Lennox, Charles Stuart, Duke of ; his birth and parentage 102 ; his character 103-104 ; a suitor for the hand of Elizabeth Hamilton, 105 ; woos Frances through Miss La Garde, 106 ; discovered with Frances by the King, 108 ; withdraws to Cobham, 110 ; elopes with Frances, 113 ; returns to London, 116 ; letter to, from Lord St Alban's, 132 ; at Cobham Hall, 133, 134 ; called away to Dorset, 135, 136 ; contemplates retiring to Aubigny, 147 ; moves to Whitehall, 158 ; receives visit from Pepys, 159 ; his financial difficulties, 165 ; his diplomatic ambitions, 169 ; aims at the office of Lord Chamberlain, 173 ; appointed Ambassador to Denmark, 187 ; his elaborate preparations, 191 ; his arrival in Copenhagen, 192 ; his ability and diligence, 193, 194 ; his private correspondence, 195 et seq ; his self-indulgence, 199 ; his continued affection for and trust in Frances, 200-201 ; his death, 203-206 ; his body embalmed, 206 ; his debts, 209 ; his body sent back to England, 213 ; his funeral, 214
Richmond and Lennox, Esmé, Duke of, 102
Richmond and Lennox, Frances Stuart, Duchess of, see Stuart, Frances
Richmond and Lennox, James, Duke of, 50, 245 note, 246 note
Richmond and Lennox, Ludovic, Duke of, 215, 245 and note, 246
Richmond and Lennox, Mary Villiers, Duchess of, 48-50, 246 note, 263
Rijks Museum, miniature of Frances Stuart at, 268
Rivers, C., engraving of Frances Stuart by, 262
Robinson, Sir J., 138
Robinson, R., mezzotint of Frances Stuart by, 267
Rochester, Lawrence, Earl of, 128 note, 240, 252
Roettier, Jan, medallist, 142, 143, 269
Roettier, Philippe, medallist, 143
Rogers, Dick, 138
Rogers, Richard, of Bryanston, 103
Rolt, Captain, 159
Roos, Lord, 221 note
Roscommon, Miscellaneous Works of the Earl of, referred to, 129
Roper, Mr, 182
Rupert, Prince, 137, 164, 177
Rutland MSS., referred to, 221, 222
Ruvigny, Marquis de, French envoy, 38-40, 144, 147, 132, 154, 155

Ruyter, Dutch Admiral, 144
Ryall, H. T., engraving of Frances Stuart by, 263

S

Sackville, Lord, portrait of Francis Stuart in collection of, 265
St. Alban's, Henry Jermyn, Earl of, 26, 132, 140, 165
St James's Park, 30, 240
St Paul's Cathedral, 96
Salisbury, 82, 84-88
Sandwich, Earl of, 12, 61, 89
Savill, Harry, 89
Saville, Sir George, 89
Schelling, 136
Scott, Lady Anne, 37, see Monmouth, Duchess of
Scroope, Lady, 15
Scriven, E., engraving of Frances Stuart by, 262
Sheerness, 137, 138
Sheldon, see Canterbury, Archbishop of
Sheppey, 137
Sidley, Mr, 179
Sidney, Harry, 89
'Sidney Correspondence,' referred to, 223
Somerset House, 23, 61, 116, 150, 155, 156, 251, note
Southampton, Earl of, Lord Treasurer, 48, 48, 89
Southwold Bay, 202
Spencer, Earl, portrait of Frances Stuart in collection of, 265
Stoop, Dirk, 8
Stowe MSS., referred to, 197, 218, 219
Strawberry Hill, 8, 266
Stuart, Lady Catherine, 102, see O'Brien, Lady Catherine
Stuart, Charles, Duke of Richmond, and Lennox, see Richmond
Stuart, Frances Teresa, Duchess of Richmond and Lennox; arrives in England, 3; birth and parentage, 4; brought up in France, 5; chosen a Maid of

Frances Teresea Stuart (*continued*)

Honour, 9; mentioned in a letter written by Lord Cornbury, 15; her friendship with Lady Castlemaine, 25-26; Charles II falls in love with, 27; Gramont's opinion of, 28; her beauty, 29; Cominge's opinion of her, 34; report of a mock-marriage between her and Lady Castlemaine, 35; her appearance at Monmouth's wedding-ball, 37; belief of French Ambassadors that she had supplanted Lady Castlemaine, 38, 39; visits the Lady at Richmond, 40; Pepys's description of her in riding-dress, 41; her popularity at Court, 43; advances made to her by Buckingham, 47-53, by Sir Henry Bennet, 53-54; her apparent frivolity deceptive, 55; affair with George Hamilton, 55-59; her freedom from arrogance, 59; resists the King's advances, 60; advised by Henrietta Maria and Mrs Stuart, 62; her cautious behaviour during the Queen's illness, 62-65; dallies with the King, 68; refuses presents from the King, 70; attends the Queen's Chapel, 71; objects to the King's interest in Frances Jennings, 73; desires to ride in Gramont's calash, 74; shuns the realities of love, 74, 75; portraits of, 75, 76; Courtin's opinion of, 79; Lely's portrait of, 84; quartered in the royal lodgings, 86; her dream, 86; commonly believed to be the King's mistress, 90; Clarendon's opinion of her conduct, 91-92; possible explanation of her virtue, 92-93; her good taste in dress, 95; at the ball on the Queen's birthday, 99; refuses all Charles's offers, 100; determines to marry, 101;

INDEX 279

Frances Teresa Stuart (*continued*)
wooed by the Duke of Richmond, 106; at the theatre, 107; discovered with Richmond by Charles II, 108; seeks the Queen's aid, 110; elopes with Richmond, 113; returns the King's jewels, 114; her own account of the marriage, 115; at Somerset House with her husband, 116; missed at Court, 131; at Cobham Hall, 133 *et seq*; rumour that she is enceinte, 134; letter to the Duke, 137-141; her affection for her husband, 141; as Britannia on the medals, 142-145; contemplates retiring to Aubigny, 147; returns to Somerset House, 150; ill with smallpox, 152; portrait of, by Cooper, 154; receives an unconventional visit from Charles II, 155-157; appointed Lady of the Bed-chamber, 158; removes to Whitehall, 158; general disbelief in her virtue, 160-161,; Mulgrave's elegy to, 162; in charge of her husband's interests, 166; her quarrel with Jermyn, 167; letter to her husband, 171-172; at Dover, 177; letter to her husband, 178-179; returns to London, 179; letter to her husband, 180-182; her escapade at Audley End, 182-184; with the Queen at Hampton Court, 184; takes part in a ballet, 185; her talent for dancing, 189; rivalry with Louise de Kerouaille, 190; her business ability, 201; beloved by Francis Digby, 201; Charles II's kindness to, 207 *et seq*; receives a present from the King of Denmark, 213; her letter to Henry Coventry, 213; her grief portrayed in verse, 215;

Francis Teresa Stuart (*continued*)
her strained relations with Lady Catherine O'Brien, 216 *et seq*; letter to Lord Essex, 218; sells her life-interest in Cobham Hall, 219; rumour that she is married to Lord Mulgrave, 219; Northumberland claimant wishes to marry, 220; her fortune increases, 221; comparatively exempt from satire, 222; her indignation with Jack How, 223; nearly always at Whitehall, 224; her fondness for the theatre, 226; patronizes Nathaniel Lee, 226; letters to Lord Blantyre, 229-230, 233-236; one of the Deponents, 239; gives a party at her house, 240; her attitude towards the Revolution, 240; petitions William III and Queen Anne, 241; her failing health, 241; correspondence about her affairs in Scotland, 242 *et seq*; attends Coronation of Queen Anne, 245; death and burial of, 245; waxen effigy of, 246-248; parrot belonging to, 248; her fortune, 248; her will, 250 *et seq*; her legacy to Lennoxlove, 252; sale of her pictures and jewels, 253; the Lennoxlove portrait of her, 254; relics of her at Lennoxlove, 255; her character, 256-259; portraits of, Appendix, passim

Stuart, Frances, cousin of La Belle Stuart, 251

Stuart, James, Duke of Richmond and Lennox, 50, 245 note

Stuart, John, 147

Stuart, Robert, 254

Stuart, Sophia, mother of Frances Stuart, 4, 10, 62, 116, 132, note, 178, 179, 251

Stuart, Sophia, sister of Frances Stuart, 4, 62, 159, 151

INDEX

Stuart, The Hon. Walter, M.D., father of Frances Stuart, 4
Stuart, Walter, brother of Frances Stuart, 4, 196
Stuart, Walter, Master of Blantyre, the original recipient of Lennoxlove, 252, 254
Suffolk, Countess of, 15, 51
Sunderland, Dowager Lady, 223
Sunderland, Lady, 83
Sunderland, Lord, 224

T

Tangier, 8, 12
Taylor, Dr, 206
Temple, 139
Terlon, French representative in Denmark, 192
'Theodosius or The Force of Love,' 226
Thomson, J., engravings of Frances Stuart by, 262, 263
Tilson, Mr, 138
Titus, Colonel, 119, 139
Titus, Mr, 179
Treasurer, see Southampton, Earl of
'Treasury Minute Books,' referred to, 212, 249
'Treasury Papers,' referred to, 241
Townshend, Lord, 186
Townshend collection, portrait of Frances Stuart formerly in the, 266
Tunbridge Wells, 42, 43, 55, 95
Turner, C., mezzotint of Frances Stuart by, 267
Tuscany, Prince of, 167

V

Van der Vaart, Jan, 262
Verneuil, Henri de Bourbon, Duc de, French ambassador, 78, 86
Verney, John, 219

Verney, Sir Ralph, 113 note, 219, 153 note
Verney Papers, referred to, 113 note, 153, 219

W

Waldy, Rev. V. E., portrait of Frances Stuart, formerly in the possession of, 266
Waller, Edmund, 145
Walpole, Horace, 8, 44, 143, 266
Warmestry, Mrs, 15
Watson, Thomas, engraving of Frances Stuart by, 262
Watts, W., 76
Wells Mrs, 15
Westminster Abbey, 214, 245, 247, 254
Whitehall, 25, 75, 79, 90, 96-98, 113, 145, 152, 155, 156, 158, 179, 224, 250
Whitelocke, Sir William, 252
Whitmore, Lady, 83
Wight, Isle of, 84
William III, 240, 241, 247, see also Orange, Prince of
Williams, R., mezzotint of Frances Stuart by, 262
Williamson, Joseph, 194
Wilton, 85
Windsor Castle, 15, 181, 229, 261 note, 267, 268
Wissing, William, portrait of Frances Stuart by, 262
Wood, Lady, 15
Worcester, Battle of, 5, 46, 232
Worcester, Marchioness of, 15

Y

York, James, Duke of, 31, 68, 69, 73, 81, 84, 88, 89, 99, 114, 167, 177, 220, see also James II
York, Anne Hyde, Duchess of, 73, 83, 84, 88, 120, 176, 265
York, Mary of Modena, Duchess of, 226, when Queen, 239

CPSIA information can be obtained at www.ICGtesting.com
Printed in the USA
LVOW10s0022181115

463081LV00001B/152/P